MARRIAGE

Love and Logic

MARRIAGE

Love and Logic

Foster and Hermie Cline

Love and Logic® PRESS Inc.

2207 Jackson St., Golden, CO 80401-2300
800-338-4065

www.loveandlogic.com

Love and Logic Press, Inc.
2207 Jackson Street, Golden, CO 80401-2300
www.loveandlogic.com

800-338-4065

LOVE AND LOGIC, LOVE & LOGIC, BECOMING A LOVE AND LOGIC PARENT, AMERICA'S PARENTING EXPERTS, LOVE AND LOGIC MAGIC,
9 ESSENTIAL SKILLS FOR THE LOVE AND LOGIC CLASSROOM, and
are registered trademarks or trademarks of the Institute For Profession Development, Ltd. and may not be used without written permission expressly granted from the Institute For Profession Development, Ltd.

Library of Congress Cataloging-in-Publication Data

Cline, Foster.
  Marriage love and logic / Foster and Hermie Cline.
    p. cm.
  ISBN 1-930429-73-8
  1. Marriage. 2. Communication in marriage. 3. Couples. I. Cline,
Hermie. II. Title.
HQ734.C5924 2005
646.7'8--dc22
                        2005002620

Project Coordinator: Carol Thomas
Editing by Jason Cook, Denver, CO
Cover design and interior design by Michael Snell,
    Shade of the Cottonwood, Topeka, KS

Contents

A Note to the Spouse Who Didn't Choose This Book

Marriage is a rite where two people, under the influence most violent, most insane, most delusive, and most transient of passions, are required to swear that they will remain in that excited, abnormal and exhausting condition until death do them part.

—GEORGE BERNARD SHAW

BENJAMIN FRANKLIN, experienced in the follies of love, remarked, *"Keep your eyes wide open before marriage, half shut afterwards."* Old Ben had a point. There are occasions we just don't want to take the time, work the hassle or discuss our differences, especially when we think, *"Hey, this whole thing was based on a mutual misunderstanding!"* One of our group participants once said, "I married Donna for more than a nighttime replacement of central heating!"

It may not have made your heart sing when your enthusiastic spouse brought you this book, perhaps out of the blue, saying, "Honey, read this! I bought this book *for us!*" Yet most of us know that our spouses read books, and sometimes urge us to participate because they want our relationship to grow. And we know that such ideas often prove valuable. After all, few of us believe we chose a dummy to relate to!

It may not sit well when someone else suggests a course of action about which we haven't even been asked for input. Such an action can become a low-grade irritation! But this time your spouse is probably right and it is likely that your marriage relationship can benefit greatly from your reading and using this book. Most of us can understand the feelings of love-at-first-sight. But few understand how to keep those feelings strong after the usual thirty-five thousand waking hours together through the first ten years. To some, that almost seems like a miracle. We want miracles to happen! We want you to remain madly in love.

Both of you really want the same thing, even if you feel quite apart from each other in some moments. You both want a close and loving relationship. Who doesn't? If you give the *Love and Logic Experiences* you will find in this book even a halfhearted commitment, we believe you will quickly come to understand how your relationship can grow through attentive communication, understanding, goal setting and problem solving. We want your relationship to blossom into a trusting bond. But we can't do it for you. We hope you'll make the commitment and stay with it.

A national speaker from Kenya, Vincent Kituku, tells a true story. From a poor family, he was seventeen before his mother bought his first pair of shoes. Things began to change after that and one day he was able to bring his family out of Africa to America. His first vehicle was a Datsun. He drove around all summer with his family, often feeling the nearly unbearable heat. Yet the automobile carried air conditioning and the button was in plain sight on the dashboard. But he was studying to be an engineer and knew that the letters *AC* referred to "alternating current." So he never thought to press that relieving button.

One day, sweltering with a friend, when asked to press it, he excitedly protested, "No, it could be dangerous! This car is DC."

"What?" his friend asked in astonishment. "What do you mean? Just go ahead and push it!"

"Don't tell me what to do in my own car!" he retorted.

Vincent laughs now. But it took him four years to work up the courage to tell the story during his speaking tours. "It was so stupid!" he says, but it was an experience that brings insight about the mistakes we can make by making assumptions and basing conclusions on them.

Could you be in this situation with the person who loves you? Could it be that your spouse is simply suggesting that you reach down and tap a button that has always been in plain sight? This book is the AC button for your relationship. Go ahead. Push it! Get ready for the cool, fresh air that will revitalize your marriage.

But remember, growth takes two and we can't do it for you! There are lots of books one person can read and share with another. Fortunate couples, happy in their relationships, can talk over those books and discuss what they say. We hope that's the kind of relationship you have. *But whether your relationship is great or shaky at times, we know that almost every couple will be able to use this book,* because all couples benefit when using this book. We provide you with concepts and exercises that are immediately useful and applicable. This is not just a read and discuss book. *This is a read, discuss, and have fun doing book!* We will help you hone your communication skills, define specific goals based on precise data and respond with specific solutions that will enhance your unique relationship.

If working things through with your spouse has seemed like a near-death experience, this is the book for both of you!

If you've read even this far, the chances are good that you and your spouse want the same thing: A loving, lasting relationship that enhances both your lives.

Foreword
Jim Fay

THE YEAR 1973 WAS A PIVOTAL YEAR for my wife, Shirley, and me. We had the good fortune to meet Foster W. Cline, M.D., a gifted psychiatrist. At that time I was the principal of a school in Evergreen, Colorado, where this very generous young psychiatrist opened his clinic.

This wonderful man gave freely of his time to help our teachers learn strategies for dealing with many of our more challenging students. He even came into our school from time to time to do demonstrations and counseling.

Foster's guidance and support in the upcoming years became a major influence in my personal and professional life. And, if truth be known, Shirley and I owe much of the success of our marriage (which is in its forty-eighth year as of this writing) to Foster's influence.

Not long after developing a friendship with Foster, we were fortunate to meet Hermie, his wife. We were impressed with their marital relationship, thinking that their marriage was the result of a perfect match. To us, here were two people so well matched that it appeared they would experience a marriage that would last forever.

As time went by, our professional relationship gave us the opportunity to get to know Hermie and Foster well. We worked together and traveled together. We also became close to their children. This close relationship, along with the Clines' openness, provided insights into their lives.

One day it dawned on us that Hermie and Foster were two very different personalities. Their marriage was not the perfect match designed in Heaven as we had originally thought. These were two people who created a great marriage because they had the tools to make it work. They learned to accept and adjust to their different ways of doing and seeing things. Now we were really impressed.

Since that time many years have gone by. Shirley and I have watched their marriage grow into a mutually loving and supportive relationship that has stood the test of good times and bad times, through raising kids, foster kids and an adoptive child. They, as have we all, experienced frustrations, outside pressures and temptations. They have even withstood the great test of remodeling houses while they lived in them. Now that's a test!

For thirty years Hermie and Foster have worked with other couples individually and in groups, in this country and abroad, helping them learn how to do the same thing: build lasting relationships. They've worked with couples by the fireside in their home, and on houseboats lashed together on America's lakes. They've worked with couples around the campfire, and in many retreat centers. The wisdom gained through all these years and experiences culminated in a book that is enjoyable and effective for couples wishing to make the most of their relationship.

One thing is obvious: No person has more impact on our individual success than our spouse. A great spouse can be either the wind beneath our wings or the molasses that we must struggle through. Love and Logic teaches that all great relationships, like life itself, don't just happen. They must be nourished. Parents with their children, teachers with their students, couples with each other must nourish successful relationships. It's almost an art form to nourish a marriage that is supposed to last a lifetime—a relationship that is often taken for granted and often filled with unrealistic expectations.

Of all creatures alive, only humans are given the expectation of choosing one mate, and cherishing that one mate for a lifetime. The problem is, we get married not because we are the same as our spouse, but because of a belief that we fit together. And the goal is to keep that fit vital and alive for seventy years. What an awesome task!

This relationship is also supposed to flower, and not just for the good times; it's supposed to flower for better or for worse, through sickness and health, with the stated promise that the only way to get out is death itself.

Foster and Hermie teach us that this daunting task is made manageable, enjoyable and exciting with this Love and Logic book. They encourage couples to explore areas of themselves and their lives that may be taken for granted, areas that are essential but seldom discussed in many relationships.

Hermie and Foster have done their best to write a book that does not simply tell how to have a more communicative and full relationship, but leads couples through the actual process in easily understandable and enjoyable steps that are bound to open new horizons of appreciation and understanding.

The DVD included with this book has examples of a couple using the *Love and Logic Experiences* in this book. They model how to handle issues correctly. Common pitfalls that need to be avoided are also exposed along with tips for avoiding them. The *Love and Logic Couples Evaluation* is an instrument that gives specific information on nine easily understood scales. Couples will share their individual views with each other, and make usable decisions regarding the strengths of the relationship and areas where each would like to see improvement.

Love and Logic parenting products introduce parents to the importance of a consultive relationship with their children. In our presentations, Foster and I often emphasize that Love and Logic concepts are universal. That universality of Love and Logic is obvious throughout this book.

The Love and Logic consultive relationship is even more important in a marriage striving for helpmate and soulmate relationships. This consultive approach is emphasized throughout the book when couples explore their communication, hopes and dreams through the *Love and Logic Experiences* that Foster and Hermie provide.

Foster and Hermie have done their best to ensure that this book encourages each individual in the relationship to be a consultant in the growth of him- or herself and their loved one. Within the relationship of a lasting and loving marriage, an individual's potential is best reached.

Read, enjoy, practice and learn from the masters, Foster and Hermie Cline. I am honored to provide the foreword to this extraordinary book.

Jim Fay
President and Cofounder
Love and Logic Institute, Inc.

Preface

Foster Cline

I MET MY WIFE AS A PICKUP. Jerry was my TKE fraternity bro. On that golden September Sunday morn in 1959, he wanted to drive around Boulder, Colorado, in his new convertible and look at coeds. I had zero—that's zero—interest in driving around ogling girls. What a total and complete waste of time! There were books to read, there was church to attend. Shoot, anything was better than driving around looking at girls. One might want to talk to them, meet them, dance with 'em and marry one of 'em someday. But drive around looking at 'em?! Life is too short.

But Jerry did have a nice new Pontiac convertible with a flat old hood that seemingly stretched to the horizon. It was like the shining deck of an aircraft carrier, spreading out in front of the wraparound windshield. There could be worse time-wasters than scooting around the campus in that.

With great reluctance to drive around looking at girls, but with a joyful anticipation of loving the golden colors of September in a new convertible,

I piled in beside Jerry, and while he was set to admire legs and shapely figures, I was excited about the acres of chrome on that magnificent dash.

And so it was that we were driving down Broadway when Jerry spied two coeds, minding their own business, walking under the canopy of elms. He said with obvious misplaced anticipation, "I'll pull over, and you ask 'em if they want a lift somewhere."

"Jerry, grow a neuron. They're not going to hop into a car with two complete strangers." It was low-grade embarrassing to even be riding around with someone stupid enough to think of pulling off a stunt like that.

In spite of my protestations, darned if he didn't pull over next to the curb and synchronize with their quickening pace. "Hey, girls, can we give you a lift?" he calls out while I slide down in the seat vainly attempting to disappear under the windowsill.

The very pretty brunette didn't give these two bozos the time of day. She kept walking. Her mother had told her not to talk to strange men, and this coed was following the rules. Her eyes were fixed on some imaginary spot blocks away, straight ahead. But the very pretty blonde looked our way, and laughed. "We're trying to cash a check, but no banks are open on Sunday. Know where we could cash it?"

"Yeah, there's a drugstore down further on Broadway that will. I'll drive you there," says Jerry with obviously misplaced hopefulness, because the brunette wasn't even looking our direction, and was picking up her pace. But the blonde was increasing the distance between them by hesitantly slowing. Then, shock of the ages, she says, "Okay, let's go." And both girls hopped into the back seat. After cashing their check, they must have realized what stalwart characters we were, because they agreed to a drive up Boulder Canyon with us. The blonde's long hair was in her face as the wind whipped around the back seat of the convertible, and realizing that the brunette was one of the prettiest girls I had ever seen in all my life, I said, "Look, there's just too much wind in the back for Nancy's hair. Why don't I pop in back with Hermie and Nancy can sit up in front with Jerry?" I guess Nancy and Jerry never really hit it off, but I dated Hermie for the first time that evening and we were married five months later. If you see a really good thing, don't let it go.

This is the way your life and marriage will always be arranged. Unexpected opportunities for fulfillment crop up dozens of times every day, we only have to take advantage of them. Some of those opportunities, like the one above, provide choices that will be life-changing. In love relationships every statement, every decision to pat our spouse on the shoulder or just walk past, every caress shared or missed, ultimately causes the earth to tremble and history itself to swing into a new pattern.

It took us a while to realize that our marriage, like yours, is not like a beautiful picture that can be admired. It is actually an ever-changing pattern of harmonizing and clashing color as God and time spin the kaleidoscope of intimate relationships. And when those colors are clashing, we've found through long experience that it's generally not good to break the kaleidoscope but to simply, with great love, faith, hope and charity, encourage it to spin into a new pattern. Years of experience with many couples have taught us that it seems to be more fruitful to learn new patterns with the same person, than stick with the same pattern with a different person.

None of you have probably ever hung around more spins of the kaleidoscope than the two of us. With time, surprisingly, we look back on the clashes and accept them more as contrasts and can laugh about them, and the harmonizing patterns grow sweeter.

Celebrate your differences. Sometimes falling off a ladder seems less painful. When both of us boarded a plane recently, a gate agent said, "You're taking your daughter on this trip?" And recently in our home a guest looked at the pictures on the front of this book and said perceptively, "Hermie has aged so gracefully." Think celebrating differences is always easy? Think again!

We had to make a decision: Which of the two pictures on the cover of this book should be prominent? We polled many of our friends. One said, "Choose the picture with the older couple. Everyone will say, if an old guy like that can make it work with a gal who looks that good, they must have something worthwhile to offer." Think celebrating differences is always easy? Think again.

And now we are anticipating the celebration of our forty-fifth anniversary, happy that we sorted out the many patterns and colors over the years and have come to this place in our lives. We feel privileged to be able to help you enjoy the colors of your own kaleidoscope.

Foster

Acknowledgments

No couple by themselves can discover the many tools, techniques, attitudes, comments, games and activities that make living together fresh, productive and enjoyable. Hermie and I would like to thank all those couples we have worked with over the years who have selflessly given so much of themselves, helping us to clarify so many of the issues we cover in this book. We wish, too, to thank Jim and Shirley Fay, with whom we have shared so much of travel, life and learning, and all the very helpful staff at the Love and Logic Institute for their encouragement as this book flowered to fruition.

And special thanks to our editors, Dwayne Parsons and Jason Cook, who both made so many good suggestions when editing our writing. Layout and cover design thanks to Mike Snell at Shade of the Cottonwood.

It is our friends, associates and clients who have enriched our lives as well as this book.

Foster and Hermie Cline

How This Book Works for You

HOW SWEET IT WOULD BE if we could just curl up in front of a fire, read a book and change our lives. "Wow! I read this book and now my whole life is different!" Dream on. It's just pesky that life isn't that way. There are some books that we can read that may make a difference for some people almost immediately. For example, the Bible is pretty darn good at changing lives, and most people who benefit from it read it over and over and study it in groups and on Sunday. *So how does* Marriage—Love and Logic *work for you?*

This is not a "read and you'll be different book." This is a lot more thrilling than that! *This is a read, think, watch, do and discuss experience.* We are going to explore the fun stuff together, the nuances of your relationship, how you communicate and how you set goals together, how you develop a helpmate relationship and how you then can evolve and become a soulmate couple together. Speaking of where you want to go, it would be a good idea to read Chapter 11 now. That's right. Right now. Put a little mark at the end of this paragraph so you'll know the exact spot to come back to. By the way, this book is supposed to be marked up by the two of you. You know, those little marginal notes and pithy comments will make this book more of a valuable heirloom for the grandkids. Mark it up! Now go read Chapter 11.

❧

Okay. Now you're back. Or are you one of those people who wants to get advice from "experts" and then doesn't do what they recommend? Shame on you! (Just kidding, but a little shame can go a long way.) Let's get started by learning about yourself and your spouse right now. Mark with a percentage all the statements below that apply to you. Then get together to see if you have agreement about how you see yourself and each other.

_____ Hey, when I'm on a roll, I can't just stop myself and turn to the end of the book.

_____ I'm a creature of habit. Who ever heard of stopping in the middle of the first chapter to read the last?

_____ Way down deep, I just don't like being told what to do.

_____ I didn't think you *really* meant it.

_____ I'm pretty compliant. My mark is right there on the page.

_____ If I'm first, I'm kinda curious about what my spouse will do.

_____ If I'm first, I know exactly what my spouse will do. And it's: _____.

In Chapter 2, we will look at very important foundation ideas and concepts. But now, in this first chapter, we want to tell you what we're up to and how we want to go about it, for however important concepts may be, simply writing words for you to read isn't sufficient for real personal and couple growth. Most people need *action, practice and mentoring* for new concepts to really sink in and become a natural part of their relationship and personality. Because the printed word alone isn't enough, we give you more. The concepts we share in print are going to come alive for you in the *discussions, experiences and interactions* you will be *sharing* with each other as you progress through this book. The real stuff of life and marriage involves action! It's not the nouns that enrich life, it's the verbs!

Everyone can benefit from guidance in our interactions and discussions. Grandma and Grandpa used to be around to give great insights: "Now Bobby, boy, you lighten up on little Missy. Ain't no call for you to say them things to her. She worked real hard to fix that breakfast for you. Hurt her feelins when you said her eggs would make them hogs sick." Seriously, extended families used to be a big help. But many couples no longer have the benefit of extended families or healthy parents to call upon for ideas. Therefore, Hermie and I want to be your extended family while you work though the specific exercises and video material here. We'll guide you through enjoyable explorations that we call *Love and Logic Experiences*. This book, like life itself, is a multimedia experience! So this book is designed around interactions to help you:

Learn concepts
Participate in *Love and Logic Couple Experiences*
Practice your new learning
Celebrate your changes

Love and Logic Experiences

LOVE AND LOGIC TIP 1
It takes more than just thinking about things.
All productive change will eventually show up
in behavior and action.

Throughout this book you will see this little picture: This represents a *Love and Logic Experience*. These are guided discussions that follow the written material and help lock in the concepts. Each exercise is designed to enhance your communication while  increasing your understanding of each other.

Knowledge by itself is sterile. As your knowledge gained through the experiences becomes translated into action, wonderful things will happen in your couple relationship. *Love and Logic Experiences* are invitations to communicative learning opportunities that you will enjoy sharing together. After all, couple relationships, by definition, must be an interactive affair.

The *Love and Logic Experiences* lock in tried-and-true, teachable, universally applicable and easily grasped techniques that best ensure long-lasting couple success. Couple concepts are easily taught and simple to understand. But just because something is easily understood doesn't necessarily make change easy! However, when these concepts are combined with the videos and the *Love and Logic Experiences* that this book offers, your relationship will be greatly enhanced. We will start with simple communication techniques, then move into more involved techniques while examining the attitudes and goals that make your relationship unique. We will look at problem-solving techniques and how to keep romance alive. We will walk you through forming helpmate and soulmate relationships.

Understanding Love and Logic concepts is only a third of the trip. Action and practice are the other two thirds. Simply understanding marriage concepts is like understanding obesity. Everyone knows about the correlation between weight and health. Yet many Americans are just plain too dumpy! Most overweight folks probably say to themselves a couple of times a week, at least, "I need to lose weight!" Likewise, couples have goals—"Our relationship needs to improve!" But such fluffy nonmeasurable goals often go nowhere. Like cotton candy, they are temporarily tasty, but quickly melt away and there's nothing left. People need measurable behavioral goals stated as fact: "I need to lose weight" doesn't cut it like "I'm going to have only salad for lunch, and exercise for thirty minutes today," which is direct, specific and immediately doable. "We want a better relationship" doesn't cut it like "We are going to concentrate on using Love and Logic terms of endearment during this discussion."

Marriage–Love and Logic will translate knowledge and understanding into immediately applicable actions for you to embed in your relationship. We'll make it easy, and enjoyable, and we will guide the way with the modeling videos. The real joy comes from practicing the techniques and learning together with your loved one. Soon the new patterns will become habits.

The Love and Logic DVD

Throughout this book you will find this symbol:

This represents the DVD found in the cover of the book. It contains videos of relevant discussions between two very enjoyable people, Rob and Amy. This DVD can be played on a home video player, as well as on any Windows computer. It is menu driven, so you can choose the short scenes that you'd like to view.

You might want to know a little background. The entire DVD was filmed one February morning in our home. We met Rob and Amy for the first time that morning. We had planned to film several couples and Rob and Amy had planned to bring their friends. However, it had snowed heavily the night before and the friends couldn't get out of their driveway. So Rob and Amy were it. They had no idea what we might require of them, but they were game to try anything. And we think you will benefit from their unrehearsed honesty, which shines through in the video segments. At first we thought that we would probably schedule another couple for a later filming. But off the cuff, with no preplanning, Rob and Amy did such a good job of demonstrating the concepts that we believe you will agree: They alone capably completed the job.

You may feel comfortable in learning a skill set by yourselves without viewing Rob and Amy's discussions. But the additional information on the DVD is most helpful. And if you feel you *might* have trouble, or if you have tried a Love and Logic skill set or a *Love and Logic Experience* and feel somehow that it could have been more productive, be sure to check out the video for that particular exercise.

The Questionnaire

The DVD also contains a website link to an online version of the *Love and Logic Couples Evaluation*. Although you can simply use and score this questionnaire directly from Chapter 7, using the website has the advantage of automatically graphing your answers so both individuals in the couple relationship can easily compare them: how you answered the questions for yourself and your perceptions of your partner's responses. The *Love and Logic Couples Evaluation* is a very important part of your couple data-gathering, and is explained fully in Chapter 7.

General Guidelines for Your *Love and Logic Experiences*

Specific guidelines are given with each exercise. For all *Love and Logic Experiences,* the following general suggestions will help you have a more fulfilling discussion:

Stick to the topic.

Good discussions are a combination of process and content exchanges.

LOVE AND LOGIC TIP 2
Be endearing: Ask questions with curiosity and interest.

Questions are often lacking when conversations go from bad to worse. We all know it is happening, and we recognize it, but we sometimes are so bound up in content that we don't slow down and give each other room to come up for air by showing real curiosity and interest in what we are doing: Questions can serve as a check on the "goodness" of the discussion as it develops. Such questions might be:

"How do you think we are doing?"

"How do you feel about ... ?"

"Is it your thought that ... ?"

Questions can be asked in a "witness stand" sort of way, with accusation and condemnation. Or questions may be asked in a thoughtful and caring way. For example, "What were you thinking?" can lead a person to feel either understood or persecuted, depending upon how it is said.

View Rob and Amy demonstrating the wrong way and the right way to have a discussion, "Poor Communication" and "Correct Communication."

We have captioned the foundation issues that best ensure couples have a productive and nonargumentative discussion. Processing while you discuss keeps you on task and on track. Rob and Amy demonstrate process questions like the following:

"How do you think we are doing now?"

"Do you feel I'm understanding your point of view?"

"Are you satisfied with the direction we are going?"

"Do you feel I'm being clear?"

"Is there something I could say or do right now to better assure you that I am listening?"

In describing these guidelines for discussion, we are giving you a taste of the communication techniques that will be more fully explored later in the book.

Terminology

This book uses somewhat loosely the terms "spouse," "partner," "couple," "marriage" and "relationship." Most couple relationships are between men and women who have or are in the process of forming or maintaining a lifelong relationship, most often within a marriage. Therefore, we are generally going to use the word "spouse" with the recognition that the concepts and tools will work for all close relationships.

With minor modifications, the skills, tools and concepts of Love and Logic can be used in all situations by humans living and working together everywhere. Couples, parents, teachers, CEOs—all are more effective when using the universal principles of Love and Logic.

A Note Regarding Authorship

When a book, as this one, is coauthored, and in it the authors refer to themselves, it is sometimes awkward to be clear on just who is writing. Generally, because Foster and Hermie collaborated so extensively, authorship is referred to with the plural "we" or "us" in most cases. However, there are times when one author is clearly referring to the other and the pronoun "I" is used. Unless otherwise noted, that "I" is Foster. Foster wrote most of the first draft, which Hermie extensively reviewed, edited and "set right." We're sure that most of you reading would have enjoyed hearing our discussions and conversations. You would have laughed and felt right at home as we hashed things out. Generally, Foster edited and deleted and rewrote just as Hermie so helpfully suggested.

Love and Logic Couples

Marriage has many pains, but celibacy has no pleasures.
—SAMUEL JOHNSON (1709–1784)

Mary Ann Is Too Soon Done Sifting Sand

Loving, lasting relationships ... talk about needing Love and Logic! It's fairly easy to have loving relationships. It's fairly easy to have lasting relationships! At times, most couples are logical. The trick is to put it all together so you can enjoy lasting, loving relationships.

Hal and Janette get married because they love each other. Each loves the characteristics they see in their person of choice. The problem is, as she becomes his wife, Janette doesn't long remain the old Janette that Hal thought he'd married. Neither does Hal continue being the same Hal that Janette married, once he is impacted by changes in his wife. Originally thinking he was wonderfully persistent, she discovers him to be woefully stubborn. He thought she was a precise piece of work, but soon discovers she is expensive and picky. Wow! Once a relationship is established, whole new personalities may emerge. It's as if couples start out on a trip to Europe, and find themselves in South America. *So happy marriages are never a destination, they are always a trip!* This book is specifically designed to best ensure that your trip is a joyful, mutual exploration of discoveries in the ever-surprising where/when of life.

People and marriages change so much that it's been jokingly said, "It's great to be married and exhilarating to find one perfect person to annoy for the rest of one's life."

A good, lasting relationship requires work, and that's not always easy. All relationships have their ups and downs. As Samuel Johnson said, marriage has its pains, but the beauty is, even if we don't like each other for a while (and that will happen), we generally hang around long enough to change our minds.

This book is designed to help you hang around with each other more joyfully and help you fall back in love quicker on those occasions when you may wonder about your original decision. It's intended to help guide you in receiving and contributing to your relationship. Of course, the more energy you invest in something, the more return you'll get back. We will help you invest wisely, effectively and enjoyably in your marriage. If you invest and participate in the Love and Logic exercises, absorbing the information we give you, you can be assured that you'll have a richer, more fulfilling and certainly more communicative relationship.

Remember the old '60s song about the boy who saw Mary Ann sitting happily on the beach playing, and fell in love?

All day, all night, Mary Ann,
Down by the seashore sifting sand.
Mary Ann, Oh, Mary Ann, won't you marry me?
We can build our home and raise a family.

Once those two get together, the days of sifting sand won't last long, that's for sure! Mary Ann starts turning a little sour and says, "Don't even mention sifting sand! I've had it with that! We've both got real jobs, clothes to wash, checkbooks to balance, groceries to shop for, noses to wipe. Gees! I can hardly remember when I had time to sift sand! In fact, I don't even see how I could have ever liked sitting there sifting sand! And if you think you've got time to hit the beach, go dig clams!"

Their relationship has changed. Relationships are living things. Like all living things, they are subject to constant change or death. The trick is having some influence over those changes, and having a peaceful understanding while life throws changes at us that we can't influence.

LOVE AND LOGIC TIP 3
You date personality, you marry character.

We meet and relate to the new person. As the newness wears off, we are increasingly impacted by the pasts that we all carry. It's a little bit of a paradox that the longer we know someone, the more we may take for granted and the less we may really understand another. Why is this? When we first meet someone, everything about them is new. That holds our interest. It makes us pay attention. We are often intrigued with all we find out. However, once we think we've found things out, our own backgrounds and responses come forward to play an increasing role in our interactions. It's hard to feel really bored or out of sorts when we are making new acquaintances. But our character shows when we're bored and out of sorts. Besides being more "us" around the other as time passes, we all change physically and emotionally. The relationship itself grows and changes. Our families grow and change.

Indeed, in our couple relationships, we blow like the sculpting wind across the ever-changing landscape of the one we love. The exciting or vexing thing is, we are both the wind! We are both the landscape! So the relationship soon gets complicated. And the landscape and the wind, both being what they are, interact to create awesome and unique relationship formations that even the Moab Desert itself would envy.

Marriage has been called a feast. It can be! But the main course should last a lot longer than the appetizer. Like Mary Ann and her hubby, you don't want the appetizer to be better than the main course!

Our perspectives change as we get older, and our personality, experiences and health all change, too. With age, we more clearly recognize that we just don't have time to waste not loving each other. Life is too short not to enjoy all the quality we can achieve. It happens so darn fast: We're kids; we marry and raise kids; our parents age and become like kids. Then we grow old and can become like kids ourselves. Then we die.

Isn't it essential to ensure real quality time? The skill sets and tools of Love and Logic will best ensure that quality.

Our middle years are important and yet tricky. In the first years we are madly in love. We can't stand being apart. That's the time Katharine Hepburn referred to when she said that a woman gets all excited about nothing and marries a man! In their later years, some couples live together, but separately. Sometimes we see such partners in a restaurant, eating together but being apart. Never looking at each other and never conversing. Perhaps some simply grow into becoming each other's silent home healthcare aide, working without pay. Not a pretty thought.

Although it may be at times partially motivating to focus on what you want to avoid, real joy in relating comes from focusing on the excitement of how you want to get to wherever it is that you are going. Most of your trip will take place in "the middle years," when some couples fall in and out of love, and cope with professional growth and child raising.

LOVE AND LOGIC TIP 4

Date and marry with a brew of hormones, lust and love,
but you'll grow old on the wine of love alone.

Don't be a Pollyanna about your time together. If you don't focus on quality time, ultimately your relationship won't be worth focusing on. And though we sometimes use the term "marriage work," *work* can be the delightful exploration of an avocation, not the obligatory effort needed for an unfulfilling vocation. The fact is, you will find these Love and Logic exercises both enlightening and enjoyable. You and your spouse will learn a lot about each other in these pages while also learning skills to apply throughout the rest of your relationship.

Is Your Home a Retreat Center?

Everyone needs a personal retreat center. We've all heard the cliché "A man's home is his castle." In reality, that's not exactly right. It should be his (or her) retreat center. Ideally, it should be a *mutual* retreat center, serving both sides of the partnership. How do you make your home a retreat center?

A home is a retreat center when both spouses love each other, compromise and show genuine concern while using attentive communication skills and setting their priorities together. That's it: Relax, talk and reach mutually agreeable conclusions.

LOVE AND LOGIC TIP 5
Accepting and capitalizing on your differences can become your greatest source of strength.

Before all else, you must recognize and accept that you are both individuals with different individual needs. Recognizing individual needs is difficult, but that's the easy part. It's *accepting them* that is the problem. And while you are recognizing and accepting your individual adult needs, the kids need constant attention and guidance along with food and clothing.

Dad has his friends and a life of his own outside the home. Mom has her friends and her own life outside the home. Both have clothes to wash and groceries to buy. School issues need attention. Either may have health problems and other family issues to deal with. This list can go on and on. The needs and demands of family life may seem endlessly intrusive and challenging. If there are no kids, we still have to recognize and plan for individual needs around professions and careers. If, in the midst of all this, a home is going to be a mutual retreat center, a guidebook is needed. And most couples don't even know they may need it. And if they do know they need a guidebook, they might not know where to find an effective one.

Let us help you build that retreat center. We can start with the simple stuff.

Whether you are the man or the woman, when you come home from a hard or difficult day, it feels good to have a spouse say, with real interest, "How's it going today, Honey?"

Even though it feels good, you understandably might respond by saying, "I don't want to talk about it" or "It's just too much to go into," but that leaves your partner feeling a little unfulfilled. However, you can still avoid giving immediate details by responding, "A lot better now that I see you!" And a simple "Hey, thanks for asking" makes the other feel temporarily satisfied. Nothing is sweeter than coming home to a loving partner who is honestly sympathetic to your problems and sensitive to your needs. But at the same time, not prying or demanding. Great friends and spouses are available but not intrusive.

Good communication almost always leads to understanding. Understanding leads to a desire to be available. It is our privilege to help you understand, communicate with and be available to your partner as you help each other grow through life.

Bring your spouse coffee in the morning and
you're "home free" the rest of the day.

Caring responses, attentive communication and perseverance in the face of difficulty are characteristics that can be learned. Some people are born with more of those characteristics than others, but we have found that almost everyone can learn the tools of Love and Logic. Without attentive communication a marriage is a union of mutual misunderstanding. Most folks are not born with good communication skills already locked inside their brain. Most men are not naturally endowed with the ability to simply hold their wives and listen when they need loving support rather than advice. You may laugh when you see Rob and Amy demonstrate this on your DVD.

Helpmates and Soulmates

A retreat center can be used for two purposes. It can be a place to simply get away from it all and relax. And that is good! It can also be a place to grow spiritually. And that is even better! We can help each other with day-to-day life and share burdens, and if we are lucky we can be a participant in the character changes of another. When couples are good at compromising and setting priorities together to reach goals, they experience the delight of a helpmate relationship. When the character of each grows from the relationship, they have a sublime soulmate relationship.

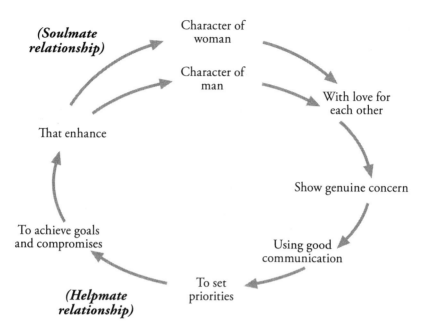

These ideas of mutual support leading through a helpmate relationship to a soulmate partnership can be simply illustrated. Above is a diagram of the relationship that is possible for all, and achieved by a few. It is simple to draw and it is conceptually clear, but the path will be filled with challenges, clefts, ravines and difficult places to ford. The diagram gives an overview of what to hope for in your marriage. It maps where the Love and Logic exercises can lead you. Does this diagram look doable to you? It is! But it is not necessarily easy nor is it a necessarily predictable path.

LOVE AND LOGIC TIP 7

When a spouse talks to us about our character, it may be hard to accept. But easier than the boss firing us.

Love and Logic will help you find and walk mutually fulfilling paths. Life can be hard, and it is such a blessing to have someone who is there to help you while you serve them. And in helping another, you paradoxically help yourself. Do you feel your appetite being whetted for the exercises you will experience, and for the great changes that can come your way?

How Do We Show Love When We Don't Always Feel It?

Kurt Vonnigut wrote that our homes need less love and more "common courtesy." Evidently Vonnigut experienced the fact that the way people show love can sure mess things up! It's not uncommon for an abusive male to say he beat up his partner because *he loves her.* Strange things can happen in the name of love! On a lesser level, a woman may nag her husband unmercifully about how he dresses because *she loves him.*

LOVE AND LOGIC TIP 8
Strive to show common courtesy.

Perhaps the best definition and description of real love is given in *The New Testament* in 1 Corinthians 13:4. Search that out if you want, but we will go there later. Before we get there we will go over the basic assumptions and attitudes that make loving each other more effective.

How Do We Communicate Attentively?

Marriage is seen as a surprising situation where women don't get what they expected, and men don't expect what they get. Seems as if there's a grain of truth in that. So, showing the attribute of attentive communication isn't just important, it's downright essential!

Attentive communication isn't an end in itself; it is the means through which we compromise by showing concern and by recognizing the special needs of our spouse. Attentive communication is the vehicle by which we set priorities and talk about goals we'd like to reach together. Attentive communication helps us walk through those stretches of a relationship, sometimes painful, where personal growth actually may best occur.

LOVE AND LOGIC TIP 9

For want of communication, the accommodations were lost.
For want of the accommodations, the goals were lost. For
want of the goals, the marriage was lost.

A man once confessed in a group session, "Talking to my wife is like a challenge course. It's hell getting over the wall, but it's so exhilarating to drop down together on the other side." He was right on. Attentive communication is the web we weave through everything in our relationships. Without this good kind of communication, the hot and sexy bloom of a new couple relationship can die of an early frost. Without this good kind of communication, most relationships are doomed.

Why? Because the couple without good communication cannot set *mutual goals*. Particularly, they can't talk about each other to each other. Generally, they simply can't openly and happily *accommodate* and *compromise* and therefore cannot attain the necessary balance of mutual growth.

Sometimes couples just don't realize they are not communicating. Poor communication is like a ubiquitous atmosphere that may be unrecognized by those in the midst of it. Of course, sometimes the lack of communication is more obvious:

Deciding that they needed a break from their bickering, Paul and Angie went to the local pub for dinner. Angie's heart swelled when, seemingly out of the blue, Paul looked in her eyes and said, "I love you to pieces."

"Oh, Honey," she replied, "I love you to pieces, too!"

Slightly irritated, Paul responded, "I didn't say, 'I love you to pieces.' I said, 'I love pizza!'"

In the following pages, we are going to spend some time helping you weave the web of attentive communication through your priorities and goal setting. We are going to show you how to reach accommodations and compromises essential to all loving, lasting relationships.

How to Set Priorities That Involve Accommodation and Compromise

Loving, lasting relationships always balance your needs and wishes with those of your spouse. And the individual needs must mesh with the needs of the couple relationship.

LOVE AND LOGIC TIP 10

Sometimes it will seem that marriage is the constant process of accommodating to a surprise you didn't expect while compromising on a situation that you wish never happened.

It is easy to feel like giving up while experiencing these repetitious acts of accommodating or compromising. Generally speaking, the martial arts teach apprentices to conquer by yielding. The Western equivalent of Judo has been said to be "Yes, dear." This is the balancing act. Marriage is the exhilaration of enjoying the trapeze, catching each other, even when the other is a bit off balance. That may be difficult, and many couples splat on the sawdust of separation and divorce. Good and lasting relationships are always a stretch. But when successfully achieved, we both grow from meeting the needs of others. Why is this?

Later in the book, we will examine how a full life must ultimately be a win/win situation. When I do things my wife's way, ultimately I will win when we win. Whenever I put my individual needs aside to make the life of another more fulfilling, the paradox is that my own life becomes more fulfilling! To give is to receive. It sounds a little crazy on the surface, but it is paradoxically true on a deeper level. Although it may be hard to imagine while in the bloom of a new relationship, compromise is the essence of lasting love.

Great sex is the ultimate situation of needing no compromise. Both should feel like they're in heaven, doing what comes naturally! No compromise, just all-out giving and receiving! Great sex can be an important part of early relationships. But it's not enough to fly very far. Someone once remarked that "getting married for sex is like buying a 747 so you can eat the peanuts." And it is understandable. Young couples seldom truly understand how much compromising and accommodating will be required for a long-term relationship that will enhance the growth of them both.

Fortunately, we have found that setting priorities and understanding each other through attentive communication is teachable. It is the logic part of Love and Logic.

Couple Relationships

Jim Fay and I wrote two books that parallel this topic: *Parenting with Love and Logic* and *Parenting Teens with Love and Logic*. We wrote them with the understanding that the principles of parenting are really the principles of leadership. We found that leadership principles stem from universal principles having to do with how people communicate, relate, carry out a mission and set goals to reach productive decisions that result in a fulfilling life. In short, we were able to show that parenting is leadership and that effective leadership is attentive communication, problem solving and goal setting.

LOVE AND LOGIC TIP 11
Ultimately, we are all responsible for taking good care of ourselves, providing choices, providing consequences with empathy and focusing on the issues that affect us primarily and directly.

The principles of Love and Logic might also be called universal principles for healthy living, because that's exactly what they are.

Hermie and I are constantly reminded of the universal applicability for the principles of Love and Logic. Wives and mothers approach us after almost every workshop to say something like, "I listened to you talk to our parenting group last year, and I've been using those principles on my husband. Now he really listens to me!"

We've heard it from husbands as well, who says things like, "I used that Love and Logic approach with my wife and you know what? I think she understands me a lot better!"

Just as the principles of *Parenting with Love and Logic* lead parents to generally raise children who are "respectful, responsible and fun to be around," so the very same principles lead to adult relationships that are much more likely to be respectful, responsible and fun to live within.

Love and Logic makes great use of one-liners to avoid arguments. Love and Logic one-liners work in marriages too. And we'll share some of those with you later in this book.

Three Basic Love and Logic Assumptions

We make three primary assumptions in this book. Over the course of teaching these principles, we've found that if for some reason you can't embrace them, the knowledge in this book won't be very helpful to you. We assume:

1. You want to understand the principles that make relationships work.
2. You want your relationship to grow and you are willing to act on the ideas and thoughts of others.
3. You understand that your relationship is a two-way street where you share the desire for loving communication, companionship and growth.

These may appear self-evident, but some of those participating in our couples weekends find, much to their surprise or shock, that their partners could not accept these three basic assumptions.

Likewise, some of you might make the mistake of thinking, "If I read this book, positive things will automatically happen." But that's a setup for a real disappointment. The correct understanding is, "When I read this book, I'll *know how* to make good things happen. Then, if my spouse and I work together, good things *will* happen." *Hoping* for something good and *working* toward something good are entirely different. It's the difference between thinking "I hope it happens" and "I can make it happen."

And even if you and your spouse think you can make "it" happen, don't assume you both know what "it" is without a good clarifying conversation. What a surprise that can be, when couples work on "it," and the "it" they are working on turns out to be different.

Here's an example:

Bob attended a weekend to prove to Patsy that he had "done every-thing" to make "it" work. For Bob, however, the weekend was, in reality, a hidden preamble to his guilt-free separation from Patsy. Patsy knew they were having trouble in the relationship, but had gone into the weekend thinking they were attending in order to make "it" work for life. She was horribly surprised to learn that he intended "it" to be a more amicable parting. It takes a commitment from both to make Love and Logic happen.

Love and Logic Attitude

To prove valuable, philosophy must be useful. It must be based on knowledge. The philosophy of Love and Logic has been tested through many families for more than thirty years. This philosophy is not about ensuring or guaranteeing the unfolding of a happy relationship. Ultimately, life is about our own growth. But in our growing and changing, we impact others. A simple little plant, reaching for the sun, can crack concrete. But its goal is not to crack the concrete! Its goal is just to reach the sun. No one can ensure or guarantee what others will do. Our part is to show you a way that will work for you individually and likely work for you as a couple.

LOVE AND LOGIC TIP 12
An indication of a healthy relationship: You know that when your partner wins, you win.

Love and Logic is not about ensuring universally successful results. Love and Logic relationships are about learning, knowing and using principles that are most likely to lead you to successful results. We hope you understand the difference between us guaranteeing it will happen (we can't) and expecting that you and your partner, like most, can take steps to make it happen.

A Tale of Two Wives

Nancy's relationship with her husband and kids is often unhappy because her husband, Brian, loses his temper too easily in his vain effort to control. Like all controlling individuals, Brian blames his wife for his and their difficulties. Consequently, Nancy is unsure of just how things ought to be in a mutually healthy relationship. She doesn't know how she "should" be acting. She therefore tends to accept his accusations and feel guilty about her "perceived shortcomings." She blames herself for the apparent lack of a successful marriage. As you can imagine, she is always stressed out.

Mary's husband, Ned, on the other hand, is equally angry and controlling. Even her kids have had some problems with delinquency. But Nancy is much more relaxed. She is much less stressed out. This is because she knows the skill sets of Love and Logic. This knowledge has given her self-confidence in the way she is currently responding to his controlling tirades. That makes all the difference in the world for her! While not very happy with Ned, and sometimes not happy with her marriage, she is much more relaxed. And she doesn't feel guilty, either. She is comforted in the knowledge that she is individually growing and doing things right at this point. She thinks, "Ned has his problems, and the kids have their problems, but that could have happened no matter who Ned married."

LOVE AND LOGIC TIP 13

In life, bad stuff always hits the fan. But it's comforting to know it's not coming from us.

Paradoxically, when we focus on individual growth and doing things right, a better outcome is more likely to occur than when we focus only on obtaining the good outcome. It's that plant-and-the-cement metaphor. It's a well-known fact in business that those companies that focus on service and happy customers generally have better sales than the companies that focus on increasing sales. Why is this?

It's Either Win/Win or Lose/Lose

The association of ALANON has long provided support groups for families of alcoholics. ALANON correctly teaches that everyone must be their own best caretaker. Putting one's self first in this loving way best ensures success. The ages-old Golden Rule tells us to love others as we love ourselves. Self-love is the standard. However, there is a big difference between selfishness and a giving love that takes our own needs, as well as the needs of others, into account.

LOVE AND LOGIC TIP 14
All interactions, including marriage, will
ultimately be win/win or lose/lose.

So if we really want our spouses and children to learn good values in doing what is right, we help them best by setting the example. It does no good to do wrong, hoping that it's right for another. Life is ultimately a win/win or lose/lose proposition. Short-term, win/lose propositions work, but they don't flourish for long. If you're winning and your spouse is losing, what's to gain? Sooner or later your relationship will dissolve. It will certainly never find balance.

On the other hand, if you do what is good for you, in a loving way, it generally will ultimately be good for your spouse, too.

There is a related example that we can give you: Hermie and I work with businessmen all over the world. Over the course of time, we have found that when a businessman puts his son at the head of the line because he favors his son, he is liable to lose both the company and the son. But when he puts the good of his company first, and sees rightly that his son must grow first in competence, both the boy and the company prosper.

This win/win proposition is an essential concept in couple relationships. Many books have tried to talk folks out of the importance of behaving as they "should" or "ought." But the *shoulds* and *oughts* are important because win/win knowledge helps us know that the happiest and most fulfilled people *want to do what they ought to do!* When I do things that make my spouse happy, I win!

It's All About Increasing Your Odds

God put the Uncertainty Principle into life to keep things interesting. The Uncertainty Principle says you can never precisely know the position of an electron; you just know it's there. Likewise, you can never know precisely how things are going to turn out, but you can be sure they will—one way or the other! One can exercise, eat right, live for health and still die an early death from cancer or some other disease. Great parents have been known to raise a child who later commits suicide. We know of spouses who have led healthy lives using attentive communication techniques, and who are basically wonderful people, yet their partners have left them for another relationship.

Fortunately, the Uncertainty Principle mainly works the other way. We might really blow something, make unbelievable mistakes and still come out smelling like a rose! But we all know inherently that the more we do things the right way, the more things are likely to work out well. Our own feeling is that all things considered, we are more likely to have things turn out well when we goof up, than to have things turn sour when we do things right. It seems as if God really does raise the odds for those doing things right.

So hopefully you see that Love and Logic is really about increasing the odds. It can't ensure success!

Life and relationships are a trip. This Love and Logic book will give you tools to help ensure a successful and lasting trip. It is a trip in which you will likely both lose or both win. Through good times and bad, the trick is to be certain you have the effective tools and techniques to increase those odds of success. You are reaching out for that elusive but obtainable win/win position that makes life really worth the living!

Love and Logic
Core Couple Beliefs

THE CORE BELIEFS OF LOVE AND LOGIC were first summed up over two thousand years ago:

> Love is patient and kind
> Love is not jealous or boastful;
> It is not arrogant or rude.
> Love does not insist on its own way;
> It is not irritable or resentful;
> It does not rejoice at wrong
> But rejoices in the right.
> Love bears all things, believes all things,
> Hopes all things, endures all things.
> Love never ends.

1 CORINTHIANS 13:4–8

Individuals in a couple relationship have their own core beliefs. Such core beliefs may go unrecognized. They may be hidden or obvious. For instance, do you believe that a good marriage is something that naturally evolves, or something that must be achieved? Do you believe that complete honesty is essential, or simply desirable? Is divorce an option or never an option? Core beliefs are tricky. They may change with experience and time.

Our purpose in this book is to clarify issues that, while obscure, may be very relevant to the workings of your relationship. We want to shed light on issues that may be unrecognized simply because they are taken for granted.

Working with hundreds of couples over the years, Hermie and I have identified eight Love and Logic core beliefs that you both best commit to for your relationship to lovingly unfold. As you read about these core beliefs below, ask yourself, "Is this something I can buy into? Can I accept this?"

Concepts that involve goals may be difficult to accept *because the goals may never be achieved 100 percent of the time.* Let's face it: If they were easy to achieve, they might not be goals! Most folks don't walk around with a goal to keep breathing ... it's automatic. But clear and straight communication may be a goal because it's not automatic for all people.

If both of you are reading this book, you already have the common goal of enhanced communication and the desire for a close couple relationship. So you are already a good part of the way there. The Love and Logic tools and techniques you will learn throughout this book are akin to the recipes in an outstandingly good cookbook. However, all the cookbooks and their recipes in the world won't help a person who doesn't want to cook! In this chapter, the two of you will learn the basics that will lead your relationship to cook.

Love and Logic Core Belief 1:
Couples must be committed to making their
marriage work.

The jokes about the difficulty of commitment in marriage go on and on. They're funny because we all recognize a grain of truth in them. We hear things like, "You can never be sure of what you are getting in marriage until you are stuck with it."

Gloria Steinem said, "Someone asked me why women don't gamble as much as men do, and I gave the commonsensical reply that we don't have as much money. That was true but incomplete. In fact, women's total instinct for gambling is satisfied by marriage."

When Ernest Hemmingway remarried the fourth time, he quipped, "Let's drink the hemlock now."

From these remarks, we can conclude that, given human frailties and human nature, your marriage *will require commitment.* Yet although commitment is a requirement, unhealthy commitment can lead to unwarranted self-sacrifice and abuse. That is a real paradox. Most of us have heard of unhappy partners who wasted their lives living in pain and psychic agony because of a promise they made in marriage. Yet commitment is an essential ingredient to lasting relationships. Why is commitment so important? It is because in every lasting relationship people will often fall out of love at times. Likewise, they may experience times when they don't even *like* each other. But marriage in which both partners are committed will hold together long enough for them to fall in love again. Affairs often break up uncommitted relationships. "As well they should," says the person who decided to leave. Affairs may not break up a committed relationship. "Hey, after all we've been through, I'm glad I stuck with you!"

Five years after contemplating divorce, after a crisis,
most couples who remain married are very glad they did.
(Institute for American Values)

Total commitment may have liabilities as well as benefits. Like almost all concepts, commitment carried to an extreme may not be healthy. A wife totally committed to stay with and honor her husband "no matter what," may give him license to repetitively give her that "what"! On the other hand, with that type of commitment most thoughtful men would be inclined to keep their helpmate happy.

Your commitment in a marriage must first and foremost be *self-centered but not selfish. Commitment to a relationship must be a mutually beneficial situation.* In a loving way, each individual must know, "I grow as our relationship grows." On the contrary, commitment to a relationship that is personally destructive becomes, in itself, destructive! *Commitment must only take place in a relationship where both people are committed to mutual growth.* When an abused wife pleads for divorce, it is certainly both deceptive and destructive for an abusive husband to blame her, saying, "You are showing no commitment to this relationship."

In a healthy commitment both must benefit from being together.

The wonderful thing is, as a relationship grows, both partners in the relationship grow and benefit. It doesn't always work the other way around. Individual growth, without growth in the relationship, can lead couples to grow apart. Individual therapy, promoting solely individual growth, can be very effective in breaking up marriages. Joe remarked, "After Angie saw Dr. Henderson, she was never again the girl I married."

True! And the truth is that if he, too, had been helped to change, and *not* remained the boy Angie married, the marriage might have had a chance. Grow together or grow apart. Those are the choices.

We commit to our relationship because a lifelong relationship with a person we love surely polishes life as little else can. Little in life is as fulfilling as growing older and wiser together. That polish provides a glow when we know that our spouse continues to cherish us, flaws and all, as the years pass. In the seasons of our relationships, it is the glorious autumn that makes apparent the nurturing that took place in the spring and summer of marriage. Too many couples split before enjoying the gold of autumn.

The real joy of closeness that occurs with growing older together simply can't be appreciated in the early years of the relationship. The perspective of time is required. Usually, young couples simply haven't had the years necessary to *look back* with wonder and appreciation upon the issues with which they have successfully coped. It's difficult for a diamond to appreciate its ultimate sparkle while it's being cut and abraded. But when we see an older couple holding hands, loving their relationship as they grow older, we know they have struggled and been polished.

LOVE AND LOGIC TIP 17

Every problem you weather together cuts a
new facet on the diamond of your relationship,
which time alone will help to polish.

Love and Logic Core Belief 2:
Males and females have differences in perceptions and needs.

Embracing the idea of equality of the sexes must not be confused with believing that men and women are alike. The differences between men and woman lie at the heart of both the joy, and conflict, in many marriages. Anna Quindlen, a journalist and novelist, once made the wry observation, "The clearest explanation for the failure of any marriage is that the two people are incompatible; that is, one is male and other female."

Equality is not sameness. Both psychologically and physically, men and women have *complementary* characteristics; they match, they fit, but they aren't the same. For instance, there is an old saying that men marry their wives with the expectation that their wives won't change. Women marry husbands with the expectation that their husbands will change. Granted that there is a lot of overlap, men and woman are just plain different.

LOVE AND LOGIC TIP 18
If you really fit each other, you're unlikely to be the same.

A round peg never fits another round peg. And it certainly doesn't fit anything with acute angles. It only fits a round hole. When inanimate objects or people fit, they are almost always complementary but different. It's not a matter of one being better or more valuable than the other, it's just that they are different. In the '70s, many people in our culture actually believed that differences in men's and women's personalities and outlooks were due almost solely to different patterns in child-raising. Boys acted like boys because they received approval for playing aggressively and with "boy toys," whatever that meant! Girls acted like girls because they were told they were chuck full of "sugar and spice and everything nice." John Gray has written about inherent differences. His book *Men Are from Mars, Women Are from Venus* would have been scoffed at in the '70s, but it was a bestseller in the '90s. At marriage workshops in the '70s it irritated some folks when both Hermie and Foster, familiar with horses, used to say, "Mares don't act like mares, and stallions like stallions, because of treatment in the colt barn!" We were saying that it's not how boys and girls are treated in childhood that leads them to believe and behave differently. It's plain old genetics.

We hope all of you can accept the premise that real genetic differences between males and females result in behavioral differences. And it's a wise couple that comes to celebrate the differences, although as this chapter implies, those differences will be irritating for you at times. For example, most marriages have one person who collects baskets and another who strongly believes the five baskets around the house are more than enough. Most marriages are a union in which one person remembers birthdays, and the other may forget them. In many marriages, one gives a Valentine's Day card that was oh-so-selectively chosen from among so many ... with such thoughtful care ... at the beginning of February no less! But the other gives a card snatched from a nearly empty card rack on the evening of February 13th. And if that last-minute snatcher is the hubby, his sweet partner is not impressed at all with the message, "Happy Valentine's Day to a great sister!"

The psychological, perceptual and behavioral differences between men and women bring no end of conflict to many marriages. Most of us, way deep down inside, think our spouses should feel the same needs, buy into the same beliefs and even feel the same as we feel, about almost everything, but especially about relationship and intimacy issues. Silly as it may sound, many husbands wish their wives thought more like men.

Professor Higgins said it pretty well in *My Fair Lady*: "Why can't she be more like me?" On the other side, many wives throw their hands in the air and say, "You know, I think *I* need a wife!"

Such conclusions stem from the mistaken idea that somehow something went wildly wrong when we married someone who is *so not us!* That notion was given credence in the 1970s, when men were urged to "tune in to their feminine side." That cultural side track caused a great deal of conflict, as men doubted themselves while searching for an increased sensitivity that just wasn't there. Somehow, no matter how the books urged them to be different, most men simply did not feel comfortable tuning in to their feminine side. It was hard to tune in to something when most men were clueless as to what the feminine side was supposed to be in the first place.

Fortunately or unfortunately, most men were not put on earth to be "a good, sensitive boy"! They may work real hard at it, but most have periods of rebellion around being dutiful. In his book *Wild at Heart*, John Eldredge argues convincingly that most men, down deep in their core, want to *do battle, have adventures and win the beauty.*

Here's another thing: for the marriage to work, as trite and as old-fashioned as it may sound, couples must continually invite each other's attention. It's the ongoing dance of courtship. It's not an ongoing courtship because you need to win the other person. And it's not because you have to do it to keep the other person. It's because that ongoing courtship helps to keep the relationship feeling alive. As the years go on, many folks forget the importance of continuing their invitation for their spouses. At that point, it's certainly easy to feel more alive with an outside relationship that provides the courtship dance. The courtship invitation says, "I want to find out more about you. Share yourself and your dreams with me." We have found that one of the major causes of divorce is a middle-aged man's feeling of lack of companionship with his wife. Separate lives without common dreams and activities can lead to an unrecognized loneliness.

Now, the courtship invitation to find out more about each other and find ways to enrich each other's life is not a simple formula such as putting whipped cream in a navel so that a partner can lick it out. (Although that might be kind of fun *once*.) Deriding such a simple formula, a writer in *Newsweek* magazine noted in November 2004:

> If I ever came home at the end of the day and saw my wife, Linnea, standing there wearing a dress and makeup and holding a martini and my pipe and slippers, I would say, "Please, Mr. Space Alien, give me back my wife and I won't ask any questions."

In writing of men's and women's natures, Eldredge rightly notes that men who pacify their wives often become pale images of the dashing man a woman really wants. She dreams of a lusty man who will shock her and sweep her off her feet with his boisterous devil-may-care boldness, but in reality may complain that her husband isn't adequately sensitive! So the woman's invitation grows cold, and the man's sense of adventure is lost to his office and e-mails. An imperceptible, almost sneaky shadow slides across their relationship, whispering to the soul of each, "It isn't supposed to be like this."

Love and Logic Core Belief 3:
Sadly, infidelity can occur. It doesn't have to end the marriage.

The pain that infidelity causes in a marriage is poignantly expressed in the following poem written by a workshop participant:

Her Eyes

Such sadness in her eyes.
Where once those brown eyes danced
With anticipation and delight in him
There now resides helplessness and defeat
Barely masking the Rage that's held inside.

What of life have those eyes known?
Love and Trust
Excitement and Expectation
Hope and Joy
Laughter and New Life
Growth and Anticipation

And then comes the Dreaded ...
Dis-ease
Dis-covery
Dis-appointment
Dis-trust
Dis-pair

The Furies are held with all her strength
At arms length.
She tries to hold onto what has been,
And keep at bay the inevitable,
Yet, knowing that nothing can ever be
The Same As It Was again.

And the work of the Devil has begun,
Gnawing away at the foundation
Of a relationship

That once was firmly rooted in
All that had gone before.
Its replacement becomes a rotting sickness
And an infinite sense of loss.
Life becomes filled with
"Why? ... What if? ... If only ..."
Compromise
Futility
And such sadness in her eyes.

To write rationally about monogamy in our basically Christian country is difficult, if not dangerous. It's difficult for us as authors. The best formula for a lasting and pain-free marriage is the same as that of a car dealer who advises, "Stick to one model and keep it forever." Everyone knows it is financially advisable to buy a car, pay it off, maintain it and keep it running. Yet so many folks feel they have to have a new car even though the old one runs fine. Remember that old "Fisherman's Wife" story of the self-destructive woman who always had to have a different house. There's something about men and women that tends to result in yearnings for something different. In that old bugaboo the "midlife crisis," a husband might be yearning for a new woman, at the same time his wife is yearning for a new house.

Problems with monogamy are everywhere, bringing down pastors and presidents. But writing sensibly about monogamy is just plain difficult. We can't do it without irritating some readers. The issue is taboo. No matter how we discuss it, or what we say about it, some of you better prepare yourselves to be offended. We've considered doing as some marriage books do, ignoring the issue altogether or simply giving platitudes! Some books simply say, concerning sex outside marriage, "Don't do it!" and let things go at that. Well, duh!

Yet the topic cannot be handled so blithely, for infidelity is the root occurrence that leads to events that shatter many marriages. Benjamin Franklin may have lived out his comment, "If there is a marriage without love, there will be love without the marriage." But even when there *is* love in a marriage the monogamy expectation can be a bone of contention and disappointment. Trust can be lost and dreams destroyed.

Monogamy for life should be seen as both a goal and a blessing. However, statistics show that this goal is oftentimes not reached. Year after year, the divorce rate holds pretty steady at between 40 and 45 percent of all marriages. Of the 2.4 million marriages taking place each year, there will be more than 1 million divorces.

Divorces

Most country western songs are "you done me wrong" songs. In fact, infidelity is so common that most preachers bring it up every month. Presidents and innkeepers have problems with it. And although in our Western culture monogamy is the goal, it must be recognized that, considering most cultures throughout history, it is the option chosen by a minority.

In our present culture and present times, many people just give up completely on monogamy. That point of view was expressed by a Hollywood actress:

Fidelity is possible. Anything is possible if you're stubborn and strong, but it's not that important. Traditional marriage is very outdated. I don't think people should live together the rest of their lives suppressing their frustrations.

Our answer is that it's really okay to be strong, and that learning to cope with frustration is usually a valuable part of growing and living fulfilling lives.

Apropos to these sections on gender differences, there do appear to be gender differences around the issue of sex. Harems of women throughout history have been much more common than a woman keeping a bevy of men. Prostitution has been called humankind's oldest profession. The basics of prostitution may be condensed to a woman saying, "Having sex with a number of men goes so against my grain, they'll have to pay me to do it." And men who respond willingly.

Social geneticists attempt to state that all creatures' behavior can ultimately be understood by assuming that genes have a mind of their own, which leads their host organism to behave in a way that will best promote the replication and survival of the genes themselves. In this view, men and women have different behaviors because different behaviors selectively enhance the survival and replication of the genes.

For females, survival of their genetics is best ensured when there is a nuclear family with a powerful male around to protect and nourish the woman and her infants and toddlers during their times of dependence. Thus, women are generally attracted to powerful men, be they presidents, basketball players or dictators. Let's be frank. Money is power, and money attracts lots of ladies.

Men are attracted to women of childbearing age. Driven by unrecognized genetic drives, men seeking an affair most often choose younger women, focusing on adequate breasts and hips, which may unconsciously indicate good odds of survival for offspring who carry on the male's genetic material.

If this theory is true, we could speculate that before the days of social welfare, women prone to have a quick and unprotected roll in the hay with a number of unknown men, produced infants that had less chance of survival. And thus that old quick-role-in-the-hay gene was a bit self-destructive and ultimately tended to extinguish itself. For most women, as noted above, sex with many males goes so against a woman's most basic values that she demands to be paid for it.

Whether or not the social geneticist's theory referred to above is correct, we have seen differences in the way men and women think about sex. We have seen a number of couples with variations on a similar theme: The couple has a poor sexual relationship. He complains that she is not receptive. She says, she can't be receptive with a person she doesn't even like! He says, "Well, dear, if we had sex, you'd like me." That is about as alien a thought as could occur to her, but it works for him!

Foster was very skeptical and doubtful when an old professor in his psychiatric training program told him about "Grandma's Rule." But as time goes on, and we deal with the behavior of hundreds of couples, we believe there may be some truth to it. Grandma's Rule states that women stray from the marriage when there is something intrinsically wrong with the relationship or the way they are being treated by their spouses; however, men will stray even when the marriage relationship is basically good. Men may have their "midlife crisis" and stray while in a good marriage with a good woman.

These gender-specific differences cause a wake of misunderstanding, pain and turmoil. She says, "What's wrong with me." He says, "Nothing." She, relating to her own way of thinking, says, "You're lying to me. Why else would you do it!" She looks in the mirror and examines in great detail her real or imagined deficiencies, while feeling enraged at him.

He says he's sorry, thinks she's making "far too big a deal" out of the whole thing, and it appears to him that she is set on making their lives miserable from here on out. He wishes she'd just go back to being the great person she was. She knows *she* wouldn't do that *unless* it *was* a big deal! She doesn't believe him when he says that the outside relationship isn't as meaningful as their own. Because she knows that, for herself, *only* if the outside relationship was more meaningful than the one at home would she probably stray. Projecting their own needs and beliefs on their spouses, some couples turn the corner toward divorce.

The Great Conflict

"So why are you seeing her? What's wrong with me?"
"Nothing, dear! You're great just the way you are!"
"You are lying to me!"
"No, really, I'm not."
"Well then why are you seeing her?"

In exploring the reasons for the pain and conflict that extramarital affairs cause in marriage, we are in no way excusing or promoting them. But understanding can go a long way. We are advocates of loving, monogamous relationships. We believe monogamy has the best chance of avoiding the turmoil and pain that often result in the dissolution of relationships that would have become richer with the passing of time. Experience has taught us that we must be realists. If the common occurrence of infidelity does occur, a marriage blessed with understanding, hard work and time will heal.

Infidelity need not end the marital relationship,
but infidelity better end!

These differences between the sexes that we have been discussing may seem valid, but if so, they are *only statistically valid.* That is, there are many men with a strong feminine side, and women with a strong masculine side. Remember, relationships are complementary. As women with a strong masculine component to their personality marry men with an equally strong feminine side, there may be complete role reversal of the issues we have discussed in these sections. While the generalizations we give are *generally* true, they are not *always* true. The issue of role reversal coming head to head with gender norms was summed up in an exchange of letters in *Popular Mechanics* magazine in May 2004:

> Just once in a while could you show a woman driving a boat or a truck. I've driven our truck over 70,000 miles, pulling a big horse trailer, while my husband stayed home tending the livestock. It would be nice if you recognized that real men don't always have to drive.
>
> *M. S.*
> *Columbia, MO*

> *I could, but I won't. You'll have to read* Cosmo *or* Redbook *to see women driving. Our readers are almost all men, so we'll be in the driver's seat for the foreseeable future at PM.—ED.*

Some great women love *Popular Mechanics.* And some "real men" may read *Redbook.* But they are not the norm! Gender differences still rule behavior.

Love and Logic Core Belief 4:
Projection causes many problems.

Freud defined and clarified the important concept of projection. It is the idea that others have, or should have, the same beliefs and feelings we have. We unconsciously project these feelings into our view of others, and are surprised or angered when they don't respond the way we would, or see things the way we do. In a recent national election, many of our friends were just absolutely flabbergasted and floored that over half the nation didn't agree with their own choice for the next White House occupant. When we wrote of gender differences in the last section, we were really touching on some specific examples of projection ... the wife's belief that her husband ought to feel about sexual issues the way she does, and his disbelief that she can't calm down and see things his way. However, the issue is more broad than one might first assume. Projection says that on almost *all* issues, "Other people should feel and think the way I think and feel ... it only makes perfect sense!" Thus, when people carry a different viewpoint or belief, there is a tendency to "shoot the messenger."

It is a wise couple (and often an older couple) who truly accept, if not celebrate, each other's differences. And the more insecure we are, the more controlling our natures can be. When control and insecurity rule, we are more likely to feel threatened by differences. Projection and the belief that others should think as we think, inevitably make our situation worse.

Men and women tend to handle personal pain and the way they solve problems differently. Men tend to go off by themselves and cope alone. Women seek out others to talk things over. Women seek other women and form bonds of closeness through the communication and mutual support they give each other in sharing their trials. Men form their tight relationships in battle or on an elk hunt. The bonds between men occur during *mutually committed shared action of overcoming*. Brotherhood is formed in the act of conquering and overcoming. Bonds of sisterhood are formed as women go through their *individual trials, supporting each other with mutual understanding.*

Rob comes home and Amy can hardly wait to talk things over with him, particularly her trials of the day. It may be around finances, kids, or other problems. When she brings it up, Rob says, "We've talked about this before. What I think you ought to do is ..."

She says, "If I wanted your advice, I would have asked for it!" He says, "Then, why are we talking about it?" She says, "*Men!*" and walks away. He thinks, "Understanding women is impossible!"

LOVE AND LOGIC TIP 20

***It surprises many to find they don't support
their spouses by giving answers. Most want
their spouse to simply listen. Really listen!***

Remember, when most people hustle off to therapy, it's because most want to be listened to more than they want answers. People pay just to be listened to. So save some money and listen to your spouse.

 Laugh and learn while viewing the videos on your DVD as Rob responds to Amy about her concerns: "The Need For Listening" and "The Importance of Listening." He may not actually be from Mars, and she may not be from Venus, but they sure can be worlds apart when she turns to him for support.

Love and Logic Core Belief 5:
Tolerance and patience are key ingredients
of a lasting relationship.

As we continue to interview successful couples in loving, lasting relationships, it becomes increasingly clear that most couples remain loving through the years not because one or the other has changed to meet their spouse's expectations; rather, their love has endured *despite the perceived "shortcomings" of the other.*

And it's not so much that one has "endured" the shortcomings, with the focus on the other, but that each has instead become less tolerant toward their own feelings of intolerance. It's more a matter of internal growth rather than a continuing focus on external change.

LOVE AND LOGIC TIP 21
Wisdom lies in becoming intolerant of your feelings of intolerance.

Jenny used to think, "Troy never picks up after himself. He doesn't put the toilet seat down. Honest to gosh, for forty years he's managed to dribble his stuff around the kitchen and bedroom. He doesn't care if there are dishes in the sink. He doesn't see that he left coffee grounds on the counter. I don't know why he can't make sure that the orange rinds go down the disposal, instead of being stuck in view in the drain!"

After a workshop, she made the conscious decision to stop hassling both herself and him about these shortcomings. Now she says, "I really don't care so much anymore. He has so many other qualities that I love. It was a waste of my energy to be so frustrated. Now I think about the fact that he brings me coffee in the morning. He even cleans the bathroom for me once in a while without my asking, and vacuums whenever I ask.

I guess if he were to keel over from a heart attack, I'd actually miss the orange peels and the toilet seat being up!"

Love and Logic Core Belief 6:
Cherish the moment every day.

Love and Logic couples are always aware that life can be far too short. They know their cherished moments can end suddenly in the screech of crumpled steel, or with the sudden metastasis of cellular metabolism gone wild. So they cherish every smile, touch and show of tenderness as something treasured in the moment.

> In the middle of writing this very chapter, while Foster was on the road, Hermie phoned in the evening, saying, "Honey, you are lucky to be talking to me. Today I was stopped at a red light, in Sandpoint at 5th and Main, and as it turned green, instead of rolling out to cross, for some reason, I checked and looked both ways. A logging truck was flying through the intersection. I glanced up to see the look of horror on the driver's face as he whooshed through, realizing what he had done. I should have been squashed flat by that truck. Only God knows why I looked before crossing with the green light."

Love and Logic Core Belief 7:
Love and Logic couples have realistic
expectations about life and love.

Let's say it like it is. Life is not always fun and relationships are not always enjoyable, not 100 percent of the time, anyway. However, by learning the attitudes, using the tools and adopting the techniques of Love and Logic, we greatly increase our chances of developing and maintaining loving, lasting relationships. That is really what life is all about. No life or relationship is meaningful and productive all the time, but it is important to have that as a goal and know how to increase the odds in your favor.

The tools and techniques of Love and Logic cannot by themselves ensure that a relationship will always run smoothly. Maybe that would be too boring! But when these core beliefs and the tools and techniques that you will learn rest in your heart, destructive escalation, painful responses, retortive statements and flat-out bad behaviors are less likely to occur. *The trick to a good relationship is in how you resolve things when the going gets tough.* Successful couples learn to understand and practice the tools and techniques of Love and Logic so that their communication with each other grows.

LOVE AND LOGIC TIP 22

Happiness lies no more in finding it than in learning to cope easily with the things that could have led you to be unhappy.

Regardless of what you might wish, or what other books might imply, a loving, lasting relationship is not built on problem avoidance, but on knowing how to handle the problems. It is not built on having a consistently caring partner, but on having a partner whose goal is to be caring. Neither is it built on being married to Prince Charming or Princess Sweetthing, but to a spouse who endeavors to understand what you consider charming or sweet.

Love and Logic Core Belief 8:
Character counts.

Personality is what we marry. Character is what we eventually live with. When we date and fall in love, we usually are focusing on the other's

51

personality. Year after year in marriage, we come to appreciate or despise their character. Perhaps it was this disappointment with character that led Katharine Hepburn to quip: "If you want to sacrifice the admiration of many men for the criticism of one, go ahead! Get married!" Character is what we bring to the relationship. Character is the interaction of free will with genetics and environment.

A well-adjusted, accepting, easygoing person is generally that way across all areas of life. If compromises are accompanied with grace and acceptance, a marriage will be much happier than one where adjustments are made with discontentment and distress. People unhappy with their lot in life are generally unhappy with their spouse.

Let's not kid ourselves. Even in a book devoted to lasting relationships, it must be recognized that divorce is always an option. And divorce may be indicated in those situations where a partner has severe *character* flaws. Character flaws are problems that are obvious and unacceptable to others; however, the individual him- or herself refuses to recognize them. Even when they are not obvious outside the family, character flaws always negatively impact personal relationships. The individual may be cold, uncaring, sadistic and outright mean, but could be the life of the party for those who are not living the hell of intimacy with the person. No one deserves a lifetime of living in fear or feeling threatened.

Although divorce is an option, it is an expensive one. Couples find out that a divorce lawyer is a lot more expensive than the minister! Plus, a divorce can set each individual back financially by about ten years. Fortunately, character can sometimes be modified through the development of a soulmate relationship. Unfortunately, that path is never easy.

If depression or mental illnesses runs in the family, then therapy and perhaps medication could be necessary. As a psychiatrist I have seen many rocky marriages where both individuals worked very hard on their relationship, sometimes over many years, only to learn *finally* that the right medication made a dramatic difference. Never discount the effect that the right medication can have on depression, rage or obsessive-compulsive characteristics. However, in this book we focus on the interpersonal issues of growth and change and on the knowledge that one's character can be greatly influenced by the people around them and the example set by a willing spouse.

Though an individual brings their character to the relationship, the relationship can change the character of each individual so that the unity of one is realized. When spouses impact each other's character successfully, they often grow together spiritually. Together, they create that rare soulmate relationship everybody wishes for but that few achieve.

Finally, genetics play a larger role than most marriage professionals like to admit. It is known that the "set-point for happiness," the likelihood of depression, ultrashort fuses, most major mental illnesses and other character traits are influenced by our DNA. In the coming chapters, the two of you will explore your backgrounds, attitudes and beliefs. These are important foundation considerations because we generally marry people who "fit" our own personalities, which were formed in our families of origin.

Couple Communication Skills

Talk Counts

Paul and Joyce went to see a marriage counselor. The way we heard the story, Paul was an old farmer with a weed hanging out of his mouth. Joyce was very unhappy with their marriage of fifteen years and complained to the counselor that Paul *never* said he loved her anymore.

The counselor, doubting, asked Paul, "She says that you *never* say you love her. Is that true?"

"Yep," came the answer. "I told her when we got married that I loved her. And if I had changed my mind, I'd have told her so."

This little story illustrates that we *say* counts. Naturally what we *do* is important. But intimacy is built on communication. There are all sorts of ways to communicate. Giving someone the cold shoulder is a way of communicating. Posture, gesture, glances ... they all communicate. But we have found that happy couples concentrate on what they say.

We saw a book for couples years ago. It was about nonverbal communication and "how to read your partner like a book." You know, it was about what it means if he glances sideways, or folds his arms, or itches on the opposite side of his face, and all that stuff.

Hermie notes, "Foster did therapy every working day for years, figuring out whether folks meant what they said or were leaving something unsaid by their nonverbal communication. But I sure don't want him to have to come home and analyze me like that! It wouldn't be fair to either of us. So we just decided to bag the nonverbal and teach our couples to say it with their mouths. No guessing. It's just too hard to relate to silences, pouts, cold shoulders and angry glances. Who wants to do that? I wouldn't wish that kind of relationship on anyone."

LOVE AND LOGIC TIP 23

Save the nonverbal communication for sugar and spice.
Deal with real issues with your tongue—none of that
cold-shoulder and pouty stuff.

This doesn't mean *everything* that sparks through a neuron has to be said. Marriage is really about being prudently honest.

We emphasize talk because most of us, even when upset, can control the words we say. But it's difficult at times to control our demeanor, our look, tone of voice or posture. For instance, if I am upset, and working things through, I might say, "Hermie, dear, I'm upset right now because ..." and appreciate Hermie attending to the "dear" and not my tone of voice. Now don't get us wrong. We are not excusing screaming or ranting. But we are saying that at times one might say something like, "You know I love you" and not sound at all loving! At that point, it helps things out if the spouse says, "I know, thanks" rather than, "You don't sound like you love me." At which point the other might reply, with increased intensity, "Well, I do" and sound even less loving.

Whether we are evaluating a relationship, planning actions, meeting goals, measuring progress or celebrating, communication weaves its web in every area. And a tangled web it can be! And nothing is so discouraging as feeling we are not being heard! And nothing can lead to arguments more quickly!

Just knowing how to listen and how to respond thoughtfully in a way that shows we are listening can avoid many misunderstandings and hard feelings. In our first years of marriage, Hermie and I had those infamous occasional "discussions." Some of them did not end very satisfactorily for me. Since I knew I was right (of course!), when my wife disagreed with me, I knew it was that either (1) she didn't really understand my point of view and all the super reasons I had to back up my position, or (2) she didn't really understand the *depth* of my feeling.

We went to some marriage groups that were offered as part of my psychiatric training. (Which was good, because the professors realized that the divorce rate among young therapists in training was pretty darn high in those days.) Hermie learned to paraphrase: She would say, "Foster, you feel the way you do for these reasons ..." and feed all my great thinking back to me! This was more like it! And then she would say, "And you feel very strongly about it for these reasons ..." She would name a few speculative thoughts. Sometimes things even *I* hadn't thought of.

"Yes!" I would agree immediately. That was great! It felt so good to know I was completely understood. End of story, right? Wrong!

Then she would say, "Would you like to know what I think?"

"Sure."

"I still disagree with you."

What??? I would stumble and reel, completely disarmed. She understood my point of view, she knew how strongly I felt, and this wise wife of mine *still* disagreed. Now I had no choice but to listen to *her* thoughts and ideas.

The beauty of attentive communication is that the techniques are teachable and quite easily learned. Some issues in a relationship may go "deeper" than inability to communicate if the problems have to do with motivation and character. But regardless of the depth of any particular issue, without attentive communication, most relationships are doomed to failure. So we have to learn to communicate effectively *first*. Once we understand the ins and outs of this important foundation to healthy relationships, we can go on to all the important stuff ... problem solving, romance enhancement, follow-up and the celebration of your changes.

Contracting for a *Love and Logic Experience*

Love and Logic Experiences can provide interactions that will result in great learning and increased closeness, or if the couple has habitual bad habits, these experiences could lead to even more disagreements and arguments. This is not likely, but possible. So if you and your partner find yourselves constantly arguing and disagreeing without resolution as you work through the exercises, then you will need to read very carefully and follow the directions in the two steps given below. If, on the other hand, you are among the few lucky couples who enjoy discussing things together, then you need only peruse these steps, as you can probably relate without them or you probably do as they suggest already.

Some *Love and Logic Experiences* differ in the depth of the issues they cover. The first *Love and Logic Experience*, "Communicating with Acceptance Using Paraphrasing," does not deal with issues of depth at all. It simply gives you practice making sure that you actually hear each other.

As you prepare for each *Love and Logic Experience*, you will want to use a format that ensures that you are both equally committed and are interacting at a time that is convenient for both of you. When one person in a relationship is excited about something and the other is less so, the one has the tendency to push their enthusiasm on the other, ignoring the other's reasons for hesitation. On the other hand, if one is reluctant about discussing or completing a *Love and Logic Experience*, they make excuses about not having time. So the steps below are designed to help you avoid difficulties when contracting for a *Love and Logic Experience*. It may be that many of you automatically take such contracting considerations into account and don't need to spend time formalizing your agreements.

View the videos about contracting for a *Love and Logic Experience*: "A Love & Logic Experience," "Discussing Paraphrasing" and "Paraphrasing Correctly." Laugh and learn with Amy and Rob. Note that it is not at all helpful when Amy enthusiastically launches into her discussion without a contract or agreement for discussion with Rob.

Step 1: Agree on time and place for your exercises.

Like all important discussions, whether in a marriage or in a business, a groundwork of when, where and how must be agreed upon by all parties. Pick a time and place and setting convenient for both. Think about the setting. Is this something we would like to discuss in the afternoon, sitting on a sofa? In the evening over dinner with candles? While sitting in the hot tub at the end of the day?

For every *Love and Logic Experience* that you will carry out together, you need to make mutually agreeable decisions about time and place. Couples who have habituated conflict have great trouble just deciding on when and where to talk about issues. By being unable to even decide when to talk, they are able to avoid talking! Paula may be able to think to herself, "The reason Bob and I have problems is because we don't make time to talk." Perhaps that is a more reassuring thought, on a subliminal basis, than, "Bob and I don't know how to talk."

Step 2: Decide on the format for your exercises.

We have found that the *Love and Logic Experiences* are more meaningful when each individual fills out answers for *Experience* questions before your scheduled meeting. Then, during your discussion time, your individual responses are free of each other's influence. However, some couples prefer to sit down with the book and the exercises, exploring the questions and answers together without prerecording their responses.

Love and Logic Paraphrasing

Paraphrasing is not "parrot phrasing." It does not come through patronization or not caring. Paraphrasing means using *different* words to show a speaker that his or her point of view is *understood*.

LOVE AND LOGIC TIP 24
Spouses need to know that they really hear each other regardless of whether or not they agree!

The reason paraphrasing is so effective is that it shows that at least *thinking* is going into your responses to your loved one's thoughts and ideas. Honestly, if couples paraphrased each other there would be a massive increase in the satisfaction level of most relationships. The value of the results that paraphrasing brings is worth the minimal time and effort that it takes to do it.

After listening to your spouse's comments, paraphrasing can often start with:

"Are you saying that ... ?"
"Are you feeling ... ?"
"Do you want me to understand that ... ?"

However, there is one trick, often used unconsciously, that can make paraphrasing ineffective: we want to respond so badly (and not just listen) that we add to our paraphrase some of our own perceptions. Let's look at some examples in which a little twist can lead to feelings of being misunderstood:

STATEMENT 1
"So when you said that 'I didn't look at all good in that dress' I felt like you were criticizing my weight."

Tacky Paraphrase 1
"So you are saying you couldn't handle straight talk about how the dress looked."

Correct Paraphrase 1
"You are saying that you are overly sensitive in areas where a statement could have to do with your weight."

STATEMENT 2
"You are always trying to jive me with your explanations and excuses."

Tacky Paraphrase 2
"You are saying that you misperceive reasons as excuses. Right?"

Correct Paraphrase 2

"When I say something that you misinterpret as an excuse, it turns you off."

When paraphrasing is done correctly, the person making the statement does not feel the need to answer something that the respondent has said, other than to say, hopefully with appreciation, "Yes, that is how I feel" or "No, I don't think you quite have it yet."

Now, when a loved one says, "I don't like your excuses," we may feel like responding, "That's not an excuse, it's simply the fact of the situation and I couldn't help it!" And one might think, "With all this paraphrasing, why can't I give my point of view?!!!" Hey, wait your turn. It'll come. The problem is, when we immediately start answering each other and giving our own point of view without paraphrasing, we get so wound up in figuring out our answers and our argument strategies that neither of us feels listened to and understood.

It's better to give our point of view *after* listening and paraphrasing, and *then* others *want* to listen. It might seem like a big waste of time, but you will find that paraphrasing has great rewards.

The steps in paraphrasing are as follows:

1. The first person expresses his or her point of view and the second paraphrases until the first person feels completely understood.
2. The second person *then* says, "Can I give you my perception on this?" and now the first person listens and paraphrases until the second person feels completely understood.
3. *Note that there may be no agreement at all at this point.* People are simply able to express themselves and *know* they are understood. Everyone feels *listened to!*

Most couples who communicate well carry out the paraphrasing steps in shorthand, with knowing nods of understanding or simple "yeahs" communicating comprehension. However, we have found that if couples have trouble listening to each other, they'd better follow the formula and *then* move to the shorthand comments. If that describes your relationship, then you'd better start with the "Do I hear you saying ... ?" routines.

Troy told us, "Man! I never realized the value of paraphrasing and really listening to Mary! What an eye-opener! She used to hit me with all these complaints about the kids and her day when I got home, and I'd have some good answers for her, but our conversations never went anywhere, and she 'Yes but'ed' everything, and I'd leave frustrated and she'd leave unfulfilled and we never quite knew where it all went wrong. Then I started paraphrasing how she felt about things, and she was so happy! It was such a shock to me! She didn't even want my answers, my great God-like answers ... she just needed me to listen and she was so appreciative, and of course she has her own answers that I'd never let her get to while I was giving my answers!"

Communicating with Acceptance Using Paraphrasing

This first experience will lead you through some revealing but noncontroversial and nonthreatening issues. It is designed to give you practice using the basic technique of paraphrasing. The added value is that you may find out new things about each other.

The goal here is:

1. To help you learn more about your loved one.
2. To practice paraphrase techniques.
3. To lay a foundation for communication skills for discussing deeper issues in *Love and Logic Experiences* yet to come.

Sit in a quiet spot where you won't be interrupted. Hold hands. Choose which of you will be the interviewer and which the respondent. The interviewer asks all the questions in the exercise one at a time as the respondent answers. The interviewer paraphrases each answer *without adding any of his or her own thoughts.* At the end of each paraphrase, the interviewer asks, "Do you feel I understand your answer?" When the respondent answers an affirmative, then you move to the next question. Allow thirty minutes for this exercise.

We expect that after completing the exercise, you are going to feel, "Wow, we understand each other and we've grown." Good communication will lead you to an increased understanding and appreciation of your spouse's point of view.

Here are the questions:

1. "Tell me about your earliest memory."
2. "Tell me about your greatest achievement."
3. "Tell me about yourself in high school."
4. "Tell me about an embarrassing moment you remember."
5. "Tell me what is most fulfilling in your life at this time."
6. "What is an aspect of your life, outside of our relationship, that you wish were different?"

View the video "Rules For Communication" to see Rob and Amy modeling this exercise.

ACCEPTING DIFFERENCES IN PERCEPTION

If you found things that you could disagree about in the first exercise, you are a very creative couple indeed! The questions were designed to be noncontroversial. That's not necessarily true with this exercise. So it might test your ability to hold your tongue regarding your own perceptions. This second *Love and Logic Experience* explores a little more deeply some of the issues we looked at when exploring the Love and Logic core beliefs in Chapter 3. This exercise's greater depth should help you understand each other's point of view a little more clearly. If you find you have no differing points of view, *lucky you!*

When you do the perceptual check at the end of this exercise, you will gather more helpful information about each other.

Use the paraphrasing tools to reach the following goals:

1. Explore and clarify differences in perception and understanding about your relationship.
2. Listen without being judgmental.
3. Accept without judgment your partner's point of view.

It would be best on this exercise, because of the perceptual check at the end, to write it out before sitting down to paraphrase. Taking turns, discuss your written answers using paraphrasing. The point of this exercise is to make absolutely sure you understand your spouse's point of view. It is *not* to reach conclusions or consensus or ensure that you both agree. Allow twenty minutes for your written responses, and another twenty minutes for private, uninterrupted discussion.

For couples who feel they have good communication and no problems with paraphrase: It is most interesting for you to start right out with role reversal in your discussion. Sit facing each other. Hold hands. Play the role of your spouse, and your spouse will explore with paraphrase the answers that you feel he or she would give.

Here are the questions:

1. What are three ways your partner shows commitment to the relationship?
2. What are three ways you show commitment to the relationship?
3. What are three expectations you have about your relationship?
4. What are three expectations that you believe your partner is likely to express?
5. How frequently and in what manner do you express to your partner that you are cherishing the moment with him or her?
6. Do you see any differences in the way you handle sexual issues?

Perceptual Check

Now answer all the questions as *if you were your partner.*

❧

We expect you've had fun learning some things about each other in the paraphrasing exercises in this chapter. And we assume that after this, whenever you have one of those "discussions" that we all know only too well, you'll make sure you slow down and take the time and energy to paraphrase before popping out your own point of view.

5

Discussion and
Problem-Solving Tools

❧

So far you have learned and worked on two basic skills for attentive communication. You have learned to discuss intimate things using paraphrasing, and you have learned to listen with acceptance of your spouse's perceptions. It's time for a bold leap forward.

Now the two of you are going to examine how you handle the basic rules of problem solving. With *great affection and love,* you are going to evaluate yourselves and each other. This will call for a bit of tenderness and may be difficult at first. Most couples find it rather easy to talk about how *another* couple functions, or discuss with each other how things are going at the office, or even how difficult the children are being, without experiencing much difficulty. But when discussing their *own* relationship, it is very easy to slip into:

Not sticking to the topic
Not listening
Being defensive

Coming through as being uncaring and unresponsive

Garbage-bagging by bringing up old issues

The list of interruptions to this process can be quite a bit longer for some couples. So before you gather data about your relationship itself, it is essential to look into how the two of you discuss and solve problems together. Discussing important issues within your relationship can be a little like exploring the depths of the ocean with a remote camera. Things formerly unseen will open up. Furthermore, your surface sea of communication skills must be calm, or you will have no stable platform for a deeper look and you will not be able to find and deal with the substantial and really interesting discoveries below the surface of your relationship.

Discussion and problem-solving rules are communication tools. Some are general and some precise; some are easy and some take practice. They are essential if you plan to plumb the depths of a relationship. In everything, you will not agree on *how* you see things, but you should at least agree on how you talk about your differing visions.

LOVE AND LOGIC TIP 25
Knowing that we disagree and how we disagree
beats being entirely clueless.

The way you discuss issues generally plays a very strong role in the level of satisfaction in your relationship.

Learning How to Respond When Your Mate Is Mad at You

This chapter contains the guidelines to responding to an upset person. But we named this section as we did because, on the whole, we have found that spouses have the most trouble when the discussion is about personal issues.

Most of us are quite good at knowing how to respond when our spouse's upset has nothing to do with us. Actually, women tend to be better at responding to a husband's upset than husbands tend to be at responding to their wife's upset. Some men fail miserably. As we have already explained, there are some differences in the way we see the sexes operate. We have also emphasized that these differences fall within a normal curve, so generalizations are only generally true. They are never *always* true, and there is overlap in the sex-determined ways men and women respond to their loved-one's upset.

LOVE AND LOGIC TIP 26

Make sure you explore your partner's feelings, thoughts and ideas before you come up with advice, suggestions and solutions.

When someone is upset, people wonder, "What should I say?" It's the wrong question. The real question is, "How do I listen?" Great therapists wonder, "How do I explore this issue" far more than they wonder how to explain or provide answers to an individual. It's easy to become defensive and answer with facts and reasons rather than continuing to explore another's feelings and thoughts when someone close to us is upset over our actions.

This brings us to an important point. What does it *really* mean "to be defensive"? I didn't really understand the term "defensive" until I was well into my professional career. For many years I thought "being defensive" meant that *someone else* was making excuses for his or her behavior. It certainly never applied to *me*. Then I realized that I was being "defensive" when I gave Hermie my *very good and thoughtful reasons*.

LOVE AND LOGIC TIP 27

Your spouse hears your reasons as excuses, your thoughts as rationalizations, unless you first recognize his/her words as reasons and thoughts.

No way did I view my reasons as excuses, and certainly, *my own* thoughts were *never* rationalizations, that's for sure! It took me a while to realize that my reasons were received as an excuse to Hermie and my very brilliant and wise thoughts were, to her, simply the tasteless draft of very old wine.

Most of us understand "defensiveness" to mean, pure and simple, what *other* people do. When a person is mad at their spouse, the other can almost always easily justify his or her action, and generally expects the other to understand. At that point, a lot of conversations go from bad to worse.

There are steps to follow when your spouse is critical of you:

- *You need to paraphrase (not parrot-phrase) your loved-one's reasons for unhappiness.* Something like, "Honey, you're saying that you're unhappy with me because I ..."
- *You need to discern whether your spouse wants to vent or solve a problem.* If simply venting, there may be nothing you can say or do, at this point. But you are still better off listening attentively. That's what a woman would want from another woman, and what most men would probably want from a friend who might be listening to them.

  On the other hand, if your spouse is angry and would like to solve the problem, then just listening won't be adequate. Our partner really wants us to participate. But even in this case, you would be wise to give your spouse the opportunity to sort out whether he or she is venting or problem solving.

  Here's how you might do that: "Honey, would you like me to just be quiet and listen right now, or are there some things that we can figure out together? Would just listening, or talking things over, be more helpful?" If the other person shouts something like, "Don't give me that psychological stuff!" or "You tell me!" it means that they still need to vent, but of course there is a limit to how long you might or might not want to listen.

Does Your Spouse Want an Apology or Understanding?

In most instances, when a spouse is angry at us about our behavior or actions, one of the following is hoped for:

An understanding of his/her feelings

A recognition of how and why our actions are irritating

An apology

Abject groveling (in the case of dysfunctional relationships)

Wanting the first three may be healthy. Wanting or expecting the fourth never is.

LOVE AND LOGIC TIP 28

Be honest: Are you sorry about the way your loved one feels or are you sorry about your action? There's a time and place for either or both.

It is not uncommon for a partner to not show understanding or to not validate the other's *feelings* because doing so would be a tacit admission of guilt, misjudgment or lack of caring. Sometimes we are just feeling contrary and refuse to show understanding. Now that's useful!

In a workshop, Dean said, "I'd never ever in a hundred years say 'I'm sorry' to Mary, because if and when I did, she'd say, 'Well then why do you do it?' And it's one of those accusatory questions that has no satisfactory answer for her. Anything I might say would lead to a bigger and better argument, so I just walk off. Of course that makes her mad, but I'm pretty sure not as mad as she'd become if I apologized and then attempted to answer her questions."

Dean is picking up on a common dilemma. In our workshops, it has not been uncommon for a man to "brush off" his partner's feelings by saying, "You shouldn't feel that way, dear," while perhaps thinking unconsciously, "If I validate her feelings, it would mean I'd be cornered into admitting that I did the wrong thing when I view the whole issue as her problem."

So you have to be clear about the value of understanding, and validating feelings without necessarily agreeing with content. *Understanding feelings is not an admission of wrongdoing.* Similarly, when our feelings are understood, stifle the impulse to say, "So why did you do it, then?"

To use a common example, when the woman is mad at the man for something he did or said and his "lack of sensitivity," he has several options in his response:

RESPONSE	MEANING
"Honey, you shouldn't feel that way because ..."	Discounting.
"Honey, I did it because ..."	Justifying.
"I can understand you feeling the way you do ..." (unsaid: "though I don't agree with it")	Understanding but not validating the other's position.
"I can understand your feeling that way and perhaps if I were in your shoes, I would feel that way too ..."	Not only understanding but validating the other's position.
"I can understand the way you feel and I'm sorry ..."	Understanding, validating, and responding with a responsive feeling.
"Please, please forgive me ..." (or variations thereof)	This will only work if there are no control or blame-game issues in the relationship.

The above responses cover the gamut from defensive excuse-making to abject groveling. Obviously, some responses are healthier than others. Begging for forgiveness tends not to work in the long run. If one is married to a spouse who demands such begging, doing so will certainly increase future controlling behavior. When there is groveling, usually both lose in the long run. Often, of course, the groveler is married to a person who demands it. Couples often "fit" each other. Those who respond with defensive excuses may be married to a person for whom no amount of thoughtful reasons would ever be sufficient. People *do* tend to "deserve" each other.

COMMUNICATION SKILLS REPORT CARD

Step 1:   Read about the basic Love and Logic communication tools below.

Step 2:   Fill out the *Love and Logic Report Card of Communication Techniques* on page 90. The instructions at the end of this section, following the tool descriptions, provide the structure you'll need to discuss your report cards together.

Below we give you eighteen tools that we have found very helpful to ensure clear and thoughtful discussions.

Love and Logic Tools

Love and Logic Tool 1:
Understanding contract: Are we going to vent or problem solve?
By definition a person who vents has a head of steam and doesn't want to be turned off. So the person vents! The ventor (the complainer) owes it to the ventee (the listener) to say things like:

"I just want to get something off my mind."

"You don't need to say anything. Just listen!"

"I'm angry and I simply want you to hear me."

Unless the ventee is chronically and realistically doing something to rile the ventor, venting ought to be a fairly rare occurrence. Some people need to vent too often. They say things like, "I need to get this off my chest *right now!*" The ventee may think, "Golly, you got this off your chest yesterday, the day before yesterday, and the day before that! How much do you carry around on your chest?"

Chronic anger has many causes. Among others it might be driven by pain, physical illness, manic-depression, genetic factors that run in families or issues stemming from childhood. In any of these cases, the person may not be venting so much as spilling over. Some individuals have an endless reservoir of anger stemming from factors beyond their control. They would find greater benefit from professional help than from spousal confrontation.

Chronic ventors seldom realize, until after their marriage ends, how destructive their chronic anger can be. One lady said, prior to the breakup of her relationship, "Of course I tongue-lash Frank. It's his decision whether or not he bleeds!" On another occasion (speaking of her tongue-lashings), she said, "Frank just needs to consider the source!" He did. He left her!

Now, let's talk about problem solving. You'll want to apply problem solving only when both you and your partner:

1. Are not angry
2. Are willing to look at the situation in a nonemotional and thoughtful manner
3. Know you both have enough time to actually solve the problem
4. Can look thoughtfully at each other's issues

It is possible for venting and problem solving to take place in the same session. A partner might need to vent for ten minutes or so, and having been listened to, feel better to the point that he or she is ready to look at the issues with less emotion. The secret of problem solving lies in using the right tools and techniques when it's appropriate to do so.

Each partner should ask self-examining questions like these:

"What am I doing to contribute to the problem?"

"What can I do that would make the problem easier for you to handle, or help you with it?"

Problem solving does not take place by looking at the other person's problem and deciding what they need to do about it. You need to look at your own contribution to the cause of the problem being expressed. Think about how *you* might change. Ask for your partner's help in changing *your* part of the problem. If you both do that, you are solving the problem!

Love and Logic Tool 2:
Don't generalize.
You are generalizing when you emit accusational phrases like:

"You *always* ..."

"You *never* ..."

Be careful what you say, because generalizations come true! Our loved ones believe us. If we say, "You *always* do this ...," even if it is not true, it begins to shape their self-image and they become more that way every time we say it!

Here's a better way to handle it: Say one partner often interrupts the other. It is much more effective to catch the person in that rare noninterrupting moment and say, "Honey, thanks for not interrupting me. I really appreciate that!"

Love and Logic Tool 3:
Stick to the topic.

When we're not sticking to the topic of a discussion, we can surmise that, more often than not, we have important but underlying issues hidden from our view. It might be content (i.e., an issue we're avoiding) or it might be a character trait developed from unresolved childhood anger. Couples caught in habitual conflict rarely stick to a discussion topic. They fall too easily into the conflicts remaining unresolved and the problems yet unsolved. If you are not able to stick to the topic, ask yourself whether fighting was the norm in your childhood. It may be a learned habit. If it is, you can break it using the tools of Love and Logic.

Love and Logic Tool 4:
Stop name calling.

Even when we change a noun to a verb, it is the same as name calling. It doesn't matter whether he uses a noun and calls her a "bitch" or uses a verb and says he doesn't like her "bitching." In either case, they are fighting words to her! Likewise, it is difficult for most men to answer thoughtfully after their partner says, "You're such a bastard!" Fighting words. Even if the verbs or nouns are true, name calling is an invitation to fight.

Love and Logic Tool 5:
Use terms of endearment and stay within "touching distance."

When you are in the middle of a fight, loved ones need to know that they are still your "honey." It is nice to say, "*Sweetheart,* the thing that makes me angry and the thing that disturbs me right now is ..."

Use terms of endearment but also remain within touching distance when problem solving. Don't try to problem solve from across the room! Touching distance means that one partner can reach out and touch the other on the shoulder (no, not the chin). When we deal with couples in a group, we may ask them to hold hands or snuggle on the couch together. One woman noted, "It's really hard to fight in our usual way in this position!" Her husband answered, "Well, then there's hope!" If things have not been going well, there's nothing to lose by getting close, so long as you are both willing.

Love and Logic Tool 6:
Discussion by appointment.

Couples will sometimes argue when they have little or no time for problem solving. The following times are not good times to enter into a discussion:

Just before leaving for work.
While your spouse is cooking.
While your spouse is concentrating on something important to them.

Sometimes when an individual says, "We can discuss this later," later never comes. We've all seen that happen. When something like this is said, a spouse would be better off to offer a definite time for the discussion to resume. This will particularly help if one of you has strong, unconscious issues that can work against ever finding the "right time" for the discussion.

Some couples can go to a therapist week after week and somehow never have time to talk about their issues between the therapeutic sessions. Not having the time is a rationalization both partners have accepted. Although they might say that they want to resolve their differences, their *unconscious* mind is fighting against their *conscious* desires and prevents their relationship from moving in the right direction.

Agree on a specific time: "Honey, what do think of talking about it at 7:30 next Wednesday night? We'll hire a baby-sitter so we can talk about this without being interrupted."

Love and Logic Tool 7:
Use the Percent Desire method.

Percent Desire is a way to quickly reach compromises. Don't use Percent Desire when compromising on "bombshell" issues. Bombshell issues require a lot of thoughtful discussion, and don't lend themselves well to quick and effective compromising. However, the Percent Desire method might be very effective when two new movies have come to town. You want to see one, but your spouse is inclined toward the other. Percent Desire works best on the issues that lead to the following silly discussion:

> "As long as we are going to see a movie, I'm willing to see *Guts, Guns and Blood.* You've wanted to see that for a long time ..."
> "Yeah but, I know you've wanted to see *Quilting Ladies Play Bridge.*"
> "Well, how much to you want to see *Guts and Guns?*"
> "Oh, I'd like to see it, but maybe not as much as you'd like to see *Quilting Ladies ...*"

Let's assume that this couple only has one car, or they don't want to each see the movie they like by themselves, and there is not a third choice they both really want to see. In such cases, Percent Desire settles the problem quickly, generally to each one's satisfaction.

To use the Percent Desire method, you both choose a number between one and a hundred that represents the percent preference for your choice. You tell each other your number, then go happily(!) to the choice of the person with the highest number.

The less trust a couple has, the more difficult it will be to use this method. Some couples banter back and forth saying things like, "You tell me your number first" or "Write it down, so you can't change it!" That's not trusting.

Percent Desire is best used on *nonthreatening* issues: "I know you would like us to both stay home, but I would really like for us to go out. Let's decide it with the Percent Desire method."

This is obviously *not* for bombshell issues like, "Okay, you come up with a percentage about how much you want the affair and I'll come up with a percentage of how much I *don't* want you to have the affair!"

Trusting occurs when you have fully accepted the idea that when your partner wins, you win. Similarly, when you win, your partner wins. Percent Desire maximizes your win quotas within the relationship. The more often you win together, the more your relationship grows. Some decisions are not either/or. For instance, in the above example, the couple might see a movie they'd both like to watch. Or, if both movies were showing at the same theater, they could split up and watch their own choice separately.

Percent Desire is just a simple shortcut for averting issues over which we wonder, "Well, how much does my partner really want this or that?"

Love and Logic Tool 8:
Don't question motivation.

When your partner does something you don't like, never assume he or she was motivated by the desire to upset you. This is very dysfunctional, and if true—if one is actually married to someone who *wants* to upset another—then there are pretty severe character issues present. Motivation is questioned when you say:

"Did you do this just to upset me?"

"Are you just trying to make me mad?"

This line of questioning invites answers that will set you up for conflict.

If a partner is actually motivated to habitually incite the other, the relationship is pathologic and counseling should be sought. Most of us will not choose to live long with someone who chooses to incite us to anger. We would not likely pick such a person on purpose! On the other hand, most of us would not consciously choose to do something simply to upset our partner. Those kinds of choices move us toward abusive and/or sadomasochistic relationships, which are much less common. The simple fact is that most folks do things that upset their loved one, thoughtlessly and not intending to do so. That's not an excuse, but the problem can be worked through as long as the relationship is not soured by needlessly questioning motivation.

Love and Logic Tool 9:
Stay in the Here and Now.

When entering into problem solving, you want to stay in the Here and Now. You want to go there and stay there immediately to keep the *content* of your discussion within a productive framework. You Stay in the Here and Now by asking your partner things like:

> "Do you feel I am really listening to you *right now*?"
> "Is there something I could say *right now* that would help you
> feel better?"
> "Let me repeat what you're saying to see if I understand this from
> your point of view."
> "Are you feeling good about this discussion so far?"

One time I had a client in my office by the name of Carol who looked at her husband accusingly and said, "Howard, you never listen to me! You never, never listen to me! Just once I wish you would listen to me!"

I stepped in and said, "Carol, what could Howard say *in this moment* that would lead you to believe he's really listening to you *right now?*" She answered, "Well, I don't know. *Right now there is probably nothing he could say.*" I couldn't help but point out, "Well, if you don't know, Carol, heaven help poor Howard!"

You can recognize Here and Now questions by the fact that they generally have answers. You'll move on to solving problems faster if you avoid asking questions for which your spouse has no answer. Avoid questions like the following, which are actually accusations hiding within questions (this is called "ripping from the underdog position"):

"Why do you try to upset me all the time?"
"What do I have to do to make you love me?"
"Why don't you ever tell me the truth?"

When the unanswerable question comes at you, your best retort is to ask, "Is there an answer now that could help the situation?" In this way, an open partner will see that an unanswerable question may be the heart of the problem.

A willing partner can be coached in the Stay in the Here and Now process. A good partner coach will help a spouse Stay in the Here and Now by saying something like, "Honey, I know you are listening, and I appreciate that. Right now it would make me happy if you could respond by saying something like ...

'I understand what you're saying, and I'll give it some thought.'
'Are you are saying that you love me as you always do and you're sorry I'm upset?'
'Are you saying ... ?'"

Please observe that when you tell your partner what you would like to hear, you are not asking for his or her agreement! You are simply asking for validation of your partner's understanding or helping him or her give a response that leads to your mutual understanding. You want your partner to understand that you understand.

Love and Logic Tool 10:
Discussion for one hour at most.

A one-hour discussion on almost any problem is enough! Freud was probably correct when he set the therapeutic hour to last fifty minutes, and it's been that way ever since! Almost anything can be resolved in fifty minutes, if it is resolvable. Partners sometimes think a discussion must be an "all-nighter." When that's the case, it's easy to avoid the issue. When an honest attempt at conflict resolution results in more than one hour of discussion (and sometimes it does), then give the problem at least twenty-four hours of thoughtful time out and begin again at another appointed time.

Hermie shortens discussions and stops repetition and garbage-bagging immediately by asking, "Sweetheart, do you have new information?" I know this little sentence is a scorcher, because it quickly clarifies the situation, shutting me up in a sort of sweet way. Sometimes I like to gnaw on an issue like a dog might gnaw on a bone. I sort of work it around in my brain and mouth, and the same words could come out over and over. I'm sure it gets a little boring listening to me present a point of view, clarify a fact, or make some essential comment for the umpteenth time. When Hermie so sweetly asks, "Honey, do you have new information?" it sort of makes me stop and reflect. You know what? I realize then that I *don't* have new information and I'm just sort of prolonging the discussion unnecessarily. I need to stop and allow time to (quietly and thoughtfully) simmer down. I can tell you, even if things aren't resolved at that point, the nonsense is lessened!

Love and Logic Tool 11:
Never attempt to problem solve when you're tired.

Many, many arguments take place when an individual is tired or physically ill. Fatigue, like alcohol or drugs, inhibits thinking and increases emotional response. A professional counselor will not even talk to a person who comes to a session after he or she has just been drinking. Only loved ones are foolish enough to try *that!* Fatigue distorts your ability to think and heightens your tendency toward emotional responses. Individuals who see their therapist late in the afternoon may not be getting as much for their money because the therapist, by that time, may be tired. Likewise, a tired client may not process or retain the advice for which he or she has paid good money.

Linda said, "Once we decided not to fight when either of us was tired, we found we had nothing to fight about! What a change that one rule made!"

Love and Logic Tool 12:
Respect refuel time.

When Paul came home from work, he was very tired. So was Nancy, a stay-at-home mom who home-schooled her kids. When Paul crossed the doorstep after work, Nancy would immediately start talking to him about her day and the children. He didn't relate well. She'd become angry and felt ignored. He became defensive and withdrew. She'd become more angry and they'd be caught in a vicious cycle and experienced many unhappy evenings.

Finally, Nancy realized the importance of giving Paul refuel time. She gave Paul fifteen to twenty minutes of time after work to lie on the floor, listen to his favorite music, eat something and read his favorite magazine. Paul told us, "When I take time to refuel, it's as if I want to put something into every pore in my body!"

Obviously he needed to recoup his energy after a long, hard day. When Paul was given time to refuel, he found he could relate very well to Nancy's conversation, and she felt the same. Of course, turnabout is fair play. Paul would take the kids on his days, and give Nancy time to refuel.

When partners in a relationship have long, hard days, they should trade off taking care of the kids and handling other menial chores around the house to give their significant other refuel time. Refueling may involve simply taking a catnap or getting something to eat. The purpose is to refresh so that each partner is alert and attentive to the couple's situation at hand.

Love and Logic Tool 13:
Use "I Messages."

An I Message is about yourself. It never puts a burden on your partner. I Messages work almost all of the time for almost everyone (although they won't work for a psychopath!). They are assertive statements about where we stand. They never are aggressive demands as to how another person ought to think, act or respond.

We leave nothing for others to argue about when we use an I Message. After its use, a conflict-habituated response from a partner could only be, "Don't you use that psychological jargon on me!" The receiving partner can only fight about the fact that the I Message was used. The message leaves nothing else at which the partner can show irritation!

Every I Message has three parts:

1. "I feel _____
2. when someone _____
3. because then I feel [become, think, experience] _____."

Notice that it does not use the accusational word *you*, nor does it tell your partner what to do. I Messages assume your partner cares and has a solution to offer.

When you begin to use I Messages they may sound phony to you, especially if you've been experiencing more "thrilling" disagreements using accusations and demands. It may even be almost boring to feel content with saying, "Honey, I have a hard time really listening when people sound so angry with me." But you know what? It works! With practice, and in due time, the use of this beneficial phrasing will become natural. Couples who employ it find that the I Message opens new vistas for expressing loving opinions and requests without resulting in battles for control.

Love and Logic Tool 14:
Contract for your partner's help in your own way.

Henry may have a problem with weight. And although his wife worries about his health, it is obvious that no matter how lovingly she says, "Henry, you are starting to look like a moving oil barrel!" it won't be super helpful. However, in contracting for help *his* way, Henry might ask, "Sweetheart, when I am about to reach for a second helping, it might help me if you asked me if I really want more." Carol, using Henry's own requested words, is in a better position to help him overcome his problem.

Some spouses are forever trying to help change their partner's ways. It doesn't work to say things like, "Your problem is ..." or "What you ought to do is ..." Usually such statements are poorly received, ending in resentment and frustration. Let your partner decide how he or she would like you to be of help with an issue he or she recognizes and wants to change. By doing this you've taken away the tension and your partner's conscious or unconscious need to defend against your perceptions and comments.

Love and Logic Tool 15:
Never try to solve a chronic problem while it's occurring.

Richard is cranky in the morning, so as Christina jumps out of bed she should not say, "Richard, let's discuss your morning attitude." One good thing about a chronic problem is the fact that we can count on it to always recur! We can wait for the perfect time to discuss and problem solve the issue. Christina and Richard will both be better off discussing her issue with him at an agreed upon time when Richard is his more usual good-natured self. For instance, it's not productive to talk to a person about their drinking when they are drunk! Christina's issue with Richard is really the same kind of scenario. Richard won't listen attentively when he's in a grumpy mood.

In responding to children, it is sometimes important to act immediately (like pulling a small child out of the street). But even then, it's best to try to solve the problem when it's not occurring. Likewise in adult relationships, *doing* something is different from *solving* the issue. For instance, Bob may not want to wait for Tracy and be late for church. He may decide to take her new car and let her come later in the pickup. However, later they may want to problem solve the issue for the future. (If he is a little reluctant, Tracy will surely insist on it!)

Love and Logic Tool 16:
Be attentive to your partner's words.

Loving, lasting partnerships are not built on your interpretations of body language and facial gestures.

Say Ralph is insecure about Peggy's desire to go back to college. Peggy wants to further her schooling because she wants more out of life, and the healthy part of Ralph actually agrees with her. However, there is a side of Ralph that feels insecure about her becoming more independent. He feels threatened somehow that her consequent increase in competence will take her away from him. So his angry reply is, "Okay! You want to go back to school? Fine! Do it! I don't care! Fine with me!" But his facial expressions and body language undoubtedly show his anger. If Peggy has really been listening to Ralph's *words*, she would say, "Thank you!" right then and go off to register. But she reacts to what she sees in his expressions. She says, "You don't *sound* like it's okay with you!" And though she is right, her words open the door for Ralph's insecure reactive side to blossom anew. Since this is an old issue, and there is no "new information," it would be better for Peggy to reinforce Ralph's healthy side by saying a simple "thank you." Peggy does not realize she is simply reinforcing Ralph's ambivalent negative feelings.

All of us have trouble controlling our tone of voice and facial expressions at times. We may look angry when we *don't* want to convey angry feelings. Although we cannot always be responsible for our tone of voice, we can be responsible for *what* we say.

Coleen noted, "When John says, in an angry way, 'Nancy, I'm not trying to make you mad,' I believe him now. It has made our life so much simpler. I used to say, 'You sound like you're trying to make me mad.' And then we'd be at it! Listening more closely to his actual words has really helped to resolve this issue!"

Love and Logic Tool 17:
Accusations and statements about another person can always be turned into questions.

Almost all accusations, demands and statements are more effectively expressed as questions. Encouraging your spouse to answer a question that is asked in a loving and nonaccusatory way empowers him or her to come up with a solution. For instance:

- "You were so embarrassing at the party" might be more effectively expressed: "Do you have any concerns about your behavior at the party last night?"
- "That shirt's too dirty to wear" might be more effectively expressed, "Does that shirt look too dirty to you?" If the spouse says no, you can always still make your statement. "Well, Honey, it looks dirty to me." You haven't lost anything by asking first and letting your spouse come to the conclusion that you've already figured out.
- "Now don't be late" can more effectively be expressed: "Do you think I can count on your being on time?"
- Instead of "Your manners are so atrocious in public!" you ask: "Honey, do you ever worry about how you appear in public?"

Loving couples ought to be able to make statements and just be direct. They don't always need to dance around with questions. But the questions, at times, may have more finesse. And if there are control issues in the marriage, passive rebellion and argument are more easily avoided. Most effective counseling works through use of questions. Try it, practice it, you may like it.

Love and Logic Tool 18:
Check how you feel about the resolution.

It may be a good idea to close your discussion by checking your mutual perceptions of how the conversation has gone:

"I feel good about this conversation, how about you?"
"Thanks for being so understanding."
"How do you think we did on really listening to each other this time?"

After both partners have read and understood the list of communication tools above, fill out the following *Love and Logic Report Card of Communication Techniques.* For each skill, you are to evaluate both yourself and your partner with a grade. If the grade is an "A" it means that the one you are rating, you or your partner, has no trouble using that particular tool. Of course, a grade lower than a "B" or "C" means that improvement is needed. Note that there is an optional third column for you to "guess" how your partner will grade *you* on each of the tools.

Love and Logic Report Card
of Communication Techniques

© Foster & Hermie Cline

	Love and Logic Tool	Grade Yourself	Grade Your Spouse	My Spouse's Grade for Me (optional)
1	Clarity on problem solving or venting			
2	Over-generalizing			
3	Sticking to the topic			
4	Name calling			
5	Use of terms of endearment			
6	Discussion by appointment			
7	Use of Percent Desire method			
8	Questioning motivation			
9	Ability to "Stay in Here and Now"			
10	Discussion within an hour			
11	Avoiding discussion when tired			
12	Respecting refuel time			
13	Use of "I Messages"			
14	Contracting correctly for help (your spouse's way)			
15	Not trying to solve problems when a chronic problem is occuring			
16	Attending to words, not nonverbal responses			
17	Turning accusations and suggestions to questions			
18	Perceptual checks on resolution satisfaction			

A = Excellent
B = Usually good
C = Could be better
D = There's a need to work on this
F = Can't swim, deep water, no life-vest

View the video "Discussing the Rules of Communication Correctly" on your DVD. You will laugh and learn. Rob and Amy do a great job of demonstrating the joys of communicating when the rules are followed, and the pain that can result when they're not followed.

At this point, don't attempt to make agreements for change. We will cover the important issue of making agreements for change in the following chapters. There you will learn of the helpmate relationship. Here, just acknowledge how you communicate and don't attempt to make changes yet. After all, what you do with what you know is an issue all to itself! At this point, you will continue gathering data and information about how you operate as a couple.

These rules are very helpful and you will be using all of them in all the future *Love and Logic Experiences.* Good luck!

Developing Goals

Mutually Established Goals
Increase Effectiveness in Every Relationship

Goal setting is an essential exercise necessary in all human endeavors. Goal setting is used across the full spectrum of relationships. Companies and bureaucracies set goals. Individuals and countries set goals.

> Jenny's goal in the marriage was to be with Howard. It really didn't matter what they did, her joy was *being* with Howard. He, too, loved being with Jenny, but an almost equally important goal was *accomplishing something—doing something productive.* Years passed and the couple spent much of their discretionary time playing cards. He hardly recognized the emptiness in his creative heart until he met Kate, who was excited about learning about computers, digital photography and painting. Kate liked *learning new things and projects.*

Many couples assume they share the same goals and in part they probably do. Both certainly want to raise their Love and Logic children to be "respectful, responsible and fun to be around." But what are the unspoken goals in raising those children?

Cynthia and David had two girls. Cynthia was both a good friend and a good mother to her daughters. She would have long conversations with them about how kids should act, dress and behave. And her girls identified with her. David loved his daughters, and was a great dad. But his goal was having companions. To his profound disappointment, he found his girls reluctant to hunt, climb or go rafting with him. Being quite overprotective, Cynthia unconsciously discouraged the things their father wanted to do with them as being either dangerous or unimportant. She would say things like, "Your dad always likes to do that dangerous stuff" or "Who wants to risk falling off a mountain?" Without consciously really meaning to, she did this just enough to make his young daughters reluctant to accompany him. David didn't push the issue. He did things with his buddies instead, ignoring how much he and his girls were missing out on a close relationship until he met James, who always climbed with his twelve-year-old daughter. At that point, recognizing his feelings of loss, David's encouragement for his daughters to accompany him became pushy and laced with frustration and exhortation. His preteen girls became more negative and rebellious and the schism between father and daughters grew deeper. Had David and Cynthia had the wisdom to communicate their needs and set goals, the family might have grown much closer.

LOVE AND LOGIC TIP 29
Assumptions are often the root of conflict.
Discuss explicitly your couple goals.

Unless goals are examined explicitly, we have a tendency to assume our spouse has the same couple goals as our own. You might think that in a company like General Motors everyone has the same goal: to make great cars. But goals can primarily emphasize quality or profit, employee satisfaction or shareholder returns. Companies put a great amount of energy, time and money into establishing goals embedded in their mission statement. Your marriage and relationship deserve no less!

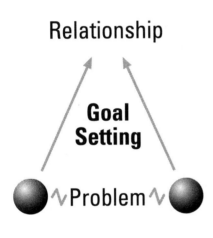

The setting of mutual goals helps especially in tough times, which either draw a couple together or pull them apart. Tough times are experienced when working through the turmoil of an affair or coping with the character trait of a spouse that melts away at the relationship like sun on a snowman. Part of goal setting includes making an accurate assessment of the present situation. *Love and Logic Experiences* will walk you through that, too.

Your Couple Mission Statement

Love and Logic Experience

A *Couple Mission Statement* clarifies goals. Every organization must have a mission that all stakeholders understand and hopefully agree upon. Successful businesses spend a good deal of effort developing team consensus around mission statements. As the two stakeholders in your relationship, develop a written mission statement clarifying the three essential ingredients:

1. The purpose of your relationship.
2. How you hope to go about achieving that purpose.
3. Possible roadblocks that could occur or are likely to occur.

Agree upon twenty minutes of uninterrupted time that you can spend together. This exercise may be explored during an evening dinner in a nice restaurant with candles burning. Sit by the fire on a cold day. Any cozy external atmosphere helps to keep the interpersonal responses warm and intimate.

Each of you should individually complete the two written forms that follow. First, on the "My Responses" form, complete the statements as you would respond. Second, on the "Perception Check on My Spouse's Responses," complete the same statements the way you feel your spouse would respond.

After completing the forms, discuss your responses. Don't forget to use your paraphrasing tools and the communication concepts you've studied. As you discuss your *Couple Mission Statement*, you may discover differences that make your discussion "interesting." (Defining your discussion as "interesting" has more finesse than seeing it as chock-full of disagreements.)

COUPLE MISSION STATEMENT: MY RESPONSES

Complete the statements as you would respond.

I see the mission of our marriage (its purposes, actions and goals) to be:

_____

_____

_____

_____

_____

I contribute by:

_____

_____

_____

_____

My spouse contributes by:

_____

_____

_____

_____

Possible roadblocks:

_____

_____

_____

_____

_____

COUPLE MISSION STATEMENT:
PERCEPTION CHECK ON MY SPOUSE'S RESPONSES

Complete the statements the way you feel your spouse would respond.

I see the mission of our marriage (its purposes, actions and goals) to be:

_____

_____

_____

_____

_____

I contribute by:

_____

_____

_____

_____

My spouse contributes by:

_____

_____

_____

_____

Possible roadblocks:

_____

_____

_____

_____

View "Your Mission Statement" on the DVD. Learn from Amy and Rob as they discuss their *Couple Mission Statement*. They enjoy each other as they reach mutually satisfying wording. They set the model of an easy, back-and-forth discussion.

FUTURE TALK

 This exercise can be great fun to focus on goals and methods of reaching them. Taking turns, one of you will be the interviewer, the other the interviewee. The individual being interviewed is to talk *as if* he or she is living in the future (anywhere from five to twenty years out). The interviewer is to ask questions about life, the marriage, the couple's goals and history, whatever the interviewer feels curious about. The interviewer might wonder what the most valuable learning experiences were over the past imagined years. When you interview, be creative. The interviewer can ask any question. *The interviewee can decline to answer any question and take a free pass.* ("That's a little too personal ... I'd like to take a free pass on that one.")

View the "Future Talk" roleplay on the DVD, and see how Rob and Amy have fun with this exercise. And, they see today's answers from tomorrow's perspectives.

THE METAPHOR EXPERIENCE

Love and Logic Experience

Most couples have a metaphor experience. A metaphor experience is some event in our lives together that sums up how our relationship functions. Alone at night, when you can't sleep, think about a possible metaphor experience and share it with your spouse in the morning. Do it now if you have some time together. Or discuss it when the two of you go out to eat. Let your mind roll easily over possible past experiences that sum up your couple pattern. Hermie and I had such an experience that we refer to now and then:

In the lake country of northern Minnesota one fall, a cousin of Hermie's had lent a small boat to a friend who lived across from the family home and dock on one of the smaller lakes. Late one afternoon, wanting the boat back, the cousin asked if I would be willing to row it back across the lake to the house if he dropped me off at his friend's place.

Of course I would. I needed a little exercise anyway, and it would be fun! Oh, how the plans of mice and men can go astray!

It was a row of some miles but one could easily see across the lake. When I started rowing, the sun was setting, spreading gold across the lake. My gosh, the evening was beautiful. As if in a trance, I rowed through that liquid gold. As the sun dropped behind the hills, it was still gorgeous, if blood red. Quickly it turned to a darker, slightly disquieting hue. Things happen fast at sunset up there in the north country, and the ripples dispersing in their quiet vees from the bow now spread as silver and black lines, disappearing into a dusky twilight. I had to keep my vision fastened on the house I had departed from to keep my bearing, as the edge of the lake was now merging into a continuous graying line along the far and receding bank of trees. Soon, the house I had departed from, the pier and the old boat-house had disappeared entirely. In fact, I wasn't really sure just where in the twilight they had hidden themselves. Up ahead on the bank of my goal, wide stretches of dark were interspersed with the flickering lights of numerous homes. There in the accumulating dark, I suddenly realized I had no idea which of those far lights indicated the location of Hermie's cousin's home. In fact, I had no idea of where the friend's home was that I had left. Obviously, if one and two are true, then three, that I had no idea of where I was, became shockingly apparent. When I row a boat, it can have a mind of its own, pointing off to the left or the right various degrees with the slightest asymmetry of the pulls on the paddle.

A number of unhappy scenes filtered through my cortex as I sat there, just me and the increasing number of stars. I started imagining what it would be like, nosing into reeds at some unbeknown marsh, getting out of the boat, sinking to my knees, if not my chin, and walking, looking like the beast of the night, covered with mud, up to someone's door to ask where the heck I was. At the least it would be very embarrassing. If I was extremely lucky, I might find a little dock and just walk up to a back door and ask directions. I was pretty sure that this would happen just prior to getting my head blown off with a sixteen-gauge shotgun. That is the by-the-backdoor favorite of northern Minnesotans.

Then I saw it. Far over on the shore, there was a blinking light. Someone was out there in the night, pointing a light across the dark, flashing it like a beacon in a lighthouse saving a ship from floundering on the rocks. "That's got to be Hermie." Or more correctly, "Please let it be Hermie." And of course, it was. She had become concerned and did exactly the right thing, guiding me home.

Throughout our marriage there have been a number of times she has flashed a metaphorical light, guiding me home from some ill-advised adventure. I go out into the night, row the boat, take the risks, and she's the one that makes it safe.

CHAPTER

7

Evaluating
Your Relationship

OUR RELATIONSHIPS AMPLIFY THE JOYS of personal and professional success. In presidential elections, the whole country recognizes the importance of the candidate's spouse. What kind of First Lady (or perhaps, in the future, "First Gentleman") will she make?

Thoughts and feelings about our loved one occupy a great deal of our psychic life. When things are going really well, and we are brimming with love and hormones, we can hardly think about anything else. When things have gone south and there are problems in our love relationship, we can hardly think about anything else. And in between these extremes, day in and day out, when our marital relationship is just floating along like the atmosphere, it is not obvious but it still surrounds. Like the atmosphere, too, if there is a little pollution or if the air of the relationship grows slowly thin, it might not be noticed until it's hard to breathe. It took the Greeks thousands of years to discover that they were surrounded by the "ether." The ether of your relationship is formed by both your history together and the way you interact. Later in this book, we'll look at goals and priorities and you will set directions for the relationship, but first, it's important to see where you are now. That's the purpose of this chapter, to help you understand were you are now so that you can more easily set your goals and priorities for the future. Think of this chapter and the evaluation of your relationship as a GPS (global positioning system) reading.

Before examining the relationship as it exists, it is wise to look back or at least take a glance at how the past is often viewed in retrospect. Generally, if we are basically happy people, and most of us are, the cracks and crevices of our past misadventures are somehow smoothed out and filled in with the sweet putty of acceptance and nostalgia. Therefore, it's surprising how our view of history changes with the perspective of time, so before you examine your relationship per se and reach conclusions about it, we would like to write a few words about the changes time will likely make in your view of your relationship issues. Some of the things that you may discover that could appear as problems or issues, even big ones, may blend out in times to come. We are saying this just to note that some of your discoveries and issues do need to be taken seriously, but maybe not *that* seriously. Your relationship is a lot like life. Take it seriously, but have fun with it. Old Man Time waves his scrawny, bony fingers, and happenings that appeared as tragedies at one time may even be funny in retrospect. And the things we took for granted filter through as being so precious as we look back.

When we were a younger couple, I started my medical internship in the Panama Canal Zone at Gorgas, the federal hospital. The very first night in Balboa, a drenching rain filled the trunk of our new car, soaking all of the carefully chosen items that we would need for housekeeping, including my medical books, until our goods arrived, via ship, six weeks later. Oh, woe. How terrible! There could have been some recriminations about whose *fault* it was that those items were left in the trunk. "Gosh, Honey, I had no idea the trunk on a brand new car would leak!" Those books were so *important.* Thirty years later we don't even remember the titles (except for the cookbook!). And we'd be happier than clams at high tide to walk together once more in a Panamanian downpour:

"What if we could do it again but we'd have to lose all the books in our living room bookcase?"

"Honey, I'd give up my entire library to walk with you again around Balboa Town in a summertime downpour."

Our son, Winfield, popped into the back seat of a new car and ripped the ceiling material as he jammed his folded metal music stand into it. Oh woe, oh, tragedy!!! Twenty years later:

"Honey, we've got to get rid of the old Chevelle hardtop. It's just sitting in the garage on blocks. No sense keeping it any longer. It's not really getting any more valuable."

"I know, Dear, but it still has that hole in the ceiling, and I just can't let it go. It just has too many good memories."

Hermie and I say, "If there are things you might laugh about later, try to start early." And that's certainly true of the issues you will discover in evaluating your relationship. As a couple, you will remember your problems, but the polish comes from the way you handle them.

LOVE AND LOGIC TIP 30

Strange as it seems at the time, your hearts will someday be warmed by the problems you faced and overcame together.

Before you get started evaluating, we want to emphasize that your relationship, like life itself, is packed with paradoxical aspects. You can take your spouse's love for granted only when you constantly give thanks for it. Now that's a paradox!

Expect to enjoy exploring your relationship. The paradox must always rest in the back of your mind. Take things seriously, but have fun. Looking at it closely can be as exciting as seeing the wings of a butterfly under a microscope.

LOVE AND LOGIC TIP 31

You relationship is a Waldo Book. Look closely, and you'll find fun little items hidden here and there.

If you want to increase your chances of real enjoyment, then you really should concentrate on using the communication tools and the paraphrasing you learned earlier. And treat each other with some tenderness on top of that. Get ready for a surprise: When you simply examine your relationship, using good communication skills, your relationship may automatically change. Your relationship works like quantum mechanics, where present theory says that simply examining a structure changes it. Honest evaluation of your relationship, how it functions and how it might improve, requires tact, at times with a bit of sensitivity for each other's feelings, hopes and desires. *How* you discuss your relationship is every bit as important as *that* you discuss it.

The *Love and Logic Couples Evaluation* you will use in this chapter is designed to help you look at and discuss specific aspects of relationship important to every committed couple. The fifty questions in this chapter will help you to better understand each other's beliefs, feelings and attitudes.

Hermie and I have found that when partners explore their own and their partner's feelings in this very specific *Love and Logic Experience*, emotions run the gamut from excitement, validation and satisfaction to outright shock as in-depth discoveries are made.

Throughout this exercise it is helpful to remember that both of you are after the very same thing. You have the same goal. You wouldn't be using this book to understand yourself, your partner and your relationship if you both didn't share the overriding goal to have a loving relationship in which you can both grow to understand each other better than you ever have before.

EVALUATING YOUR RELATIONSHIP

The *Love and Logic Couples Evaluation* helps both partners clarify and discuss:

- Overall satisfaction
- Satisfaction with specifics
- Satisfaction with work
- Satisfaction with partner
- Partner's perceived satisfaction with the couple relationship
- Communication skills
- Satisfaction with self
- Satisfaction with your diet and health
- Indications of substance abuse (including alcohol)

These are important issues. Don't rush it. Give yourselves adequate time to fill out the questionnaire thoughtfully. We recommend half an hour of uninterrupted time. We also think it is best for you to take time alone, separately from each other, to answer these questions. Some couples, however, find that writing the answers out ahead of time is unnecessary. They simply ask each other the questions and discuss the answers between themselves.

When you have completed the questionnaire, you will come together again to discuss your answers using the paraphrasing techniques you practiced earlier. By preparing your answers in advance, you are more likely to stay on topic and not stray.

In the right-hand column of the questionnaire you have choices! It is labeled "special" and there are a number of ways the two of you can decide to fill out that column. It is an enrichment column: It clarifies how well your spouse understands how you think and feel. There are a number of ways you can use the enrichment column. Take your pick:

- My guess as to how my partner will answer this.
- My guess as to how my partner thinks I will answer this.
- Answers that I wish to mark as very important for us to explore.
- Answer this question as it would have been answered by my teen, mother, or father.

Scoring procedures are described after the questionnaire.

The DVD also contains a link to this evaluation, which has the advantage of automatically graphing your answers so both individuals in the couple relationship can easily compare them. See "Link to Love and Logic Couples Evaluation" on the DVD or visit www.loveandlogic.com/marriage.

LOVE AND LOGIC COUPLES EVALUATION

For each of the following fifty statements, rate yourself 1 to 10:

10 = Perfect agreement with the statement

1 = No agreement with the statement

Question	My Answer (1–10)	Special (1–10)
1 I am satisfied with my partner.	_____	_____
2 My partner is satisfied with me.	_____	_____
3 I am satisfied with my sexual performance.	_____	_____
4 I exercise enough.	_____	_____
5 I am assertive with my partner.	_____	_____
6 I am not overly aggressive with my partner.	_____	_____
7 I receive enough affection.	_____	_____
8 I am satisfied with my spiritual life.	_____	_____
9 I eat the right amounts of food.	_____	_____
10 I allow myself enough relaxation time each day.	_____	_____
11 I don't smoke.	_____	_____
12 I have good, communicative friendships.	_____	_____
13 I don't lose my temper easily.	_____	_____
14 I restrict myself to reasonable workloads.	_____	_____
15 I don't tend to hold grudges.	_____	_____
16 My partner does not consider me a workaholic.	_____	_____
17 I live life to the fullest.	_____	_____
18 I give myself enough vacations.	_____	_____
19 I eat the right foods.	_____	_____
20 I only drink when I want to, not because I feel I need a shot.	_____	_____
21 I am upfront about my gripes and disappointments in others.	_____	_____

22 I don't tend to pout.

23 I don't hold things in too much for my own good.

24 I agree with my partner on most important issues.

25 I don't abuse nonprescription or
prescription drugs.

26 I am satisfied with myself overall.

27 I find work satisfying.

28 I feel competent in my job.

29 I am comfortable with my partner.

30 I spend money wisely.

31 I work well with my associates.

32 I communicate well with those I love.

33 My partner feels I spend money wisely.

34 I find my life satisfying.

35 I have hobbies or outside interests that I enjoy.

36 I tend to appreciate every day.

37 I am happy with my religious behaviors.

38 My partner is happy with the way
I communicate.

39 I am no more than a moderate drinker.

40 I don't generally get frustrated.

41 If I were to die today, I'd feel satisfied with
the way I'd lived my life.

42 My partner understands me.

43 I have my priorities straight.

44 I have a feeling of belonging.

45 I feel okay much of the time.

46 I can easily handle being alone with myself.

47 Most major areas of my life are going well.

48 I am generally a relaxed person.

49 I love life, overall.

50 My health is good.

Scoring the Scales

The question numbers that add to the nine scales are noted below. Add your score on each of the *question numbers* listed below to obtain a total scale score. Then, as indicated, divide your total score by the number of questions in the scale to calculate an overall satisfaction score (1–10) for the scale itself.

Global Satisfaction: 17+26+34+36+41+43+44+46+49 = _____ /9 = _____

Satisfaction with
Specifics: 8+10+14+18+30+35+37 = _____ /7 = _____

Satisfaction with Work: 27+28+31 = _____ /3 = _____

Satisfaction with Partner: 1+7+24+29 =_____ /4 = _____

Partner's Perceived
Satisfaction with Us: 2+16+33+38+42 = _____ /5 = _____

Communication Skills: 5+12+21+32 = _____ /4 = _____

Satisfaction with Self: 3+6+13+15+22+23+40+45+47+48 = _____ /10 = _____

Satisfaction with Your
Diet and Health: 4+9+19+50 = _____ /4 = _____

Indications of Substance
Abuse (includes alcohol):   11+20+25+39 = _____ /4 = _____

Discussing This Exercise

LOVE AND LOGIC TIP 32
The way you discuss the evaluation is more important than filling it out in the first place!

Okay, you've answered the questions. Now comes the important part. You've hitched the horses. Now you need to pull the hay wagon.

Within the next few days, during a mutually agreed upon quiet half-hour or so (longer if you both agree), and without rushing your discussion, go over the answers with your partner. Now is the time to put all those couple communication skills to work. It might be a good idea to look over that report card from Chapter 5 just to remind yourself of your areas of strength and the potholes that could possibly hang you up. Concentrate on having fun while you paraphrase, use perceptual checks ("How do you think we're doing?") and stick to the topic. And of course, don't discuss this at the end of the day when you are both tired.

Most couples don't cover all the answers in one sitting. This is a time for understanding each other, not getting into defensive arguments or attempts to fix the problem. There will be plenty of time later to use Love and Logic tools to problem solve issues you would like to explore.

Not that most of you would ever do it, but there are ways that couples who make a habit of conflict have been able to turn this exercise into a bad experience. Let's look at these to make sure you don't go there:

- Plow ahead without getting a good contract from your partner.
- Argue about your partner's answers and try to get him or her to change them.
- Make comments that will lead to your partner feeling guilty or angry about his or her responses.

Specifically, let's look at responses during this exercise that could be unhelpful and comments that could be substituted that would be more helpful:

Tacky Comment	Love and Logic Solution
"I can't believe you see it that way!"	"Your answer surprises me."
"That's just not true!"	"This is one of the things we see differently."
"How in the world can you think I'm happy about the way you communicate?"	"Maybe this is one we should discuss."
"You do not take good care of yourself. How can you say you are happy with your health?"	"So a heart attack would come as a real surprise?"
"What do you mean, you eat the right amounts of food?!"	"That reminds me, we need a scale."

View "Evaluating Your Relationship" on the DVD. Rob and Amy do a great job of demonstrating the joy that comes with discovery. They show, too, how one's perceptions may be modified as the partner is better understood. As we are now getting into real issues in the relationship, poor communication techniques and habitual patterns of argument can occur. Viewing the videos on the disc will help to ensure that your experience is positive.

EVALUATING OUR ATTRIBUTES

Do you see yourself as your loved one sees you? The purpose of this exercise is simply twofold. How do you see yourself? and Does your spouse think you're accurate and being honest with yourself? Occasionally there is massive disagreement. Then you better have someone who knows you very well provide some feedback.

Attributes are the actual qualities that form our personality. We act on the attributes we have, and others interact with us based on the attributes they see in us. Healthy individuals tend to view their attributes accurately. And they are more likely to perceive others accurately, too.

LOVE AND LOGIC TIP 33
Our world works smoother when we see our attributes as our spouse sees them.

The attribute issue is important because of the ubiquitous old Freudian concept of projection. Often, the attributes we see in others are the attributes we secretly, or openly, acknowledge in ourselves. Think about it. Recall that sometimes people send us the nicest cards. Or they say the nicest things. They say how generous, thoughtful or caring we may be. How fun or helpful we are to be around. But you know what? It's almost always true of them, too. So the next time you see a politician badmouthing someone else for some attribute or character trait, look for it in the speaker. Richard Nixon ran on the "law and order" ticket, only to break the law himself. Ronald Reagan constantly talked about how great the American people were, and now most people believe that he himself was great.

Of course, all positive attitudes can have their dark side if carried too far. Perseverance may slide into stubbornness, acceptance of others into naiveté, precision into compulsivity and healthy certainty into destructive rigidity.

If negative attributes are found, you need to give each other quick encouragement and ideas on how you might help each other reach the bright side of that attribute. There is a closely related positive expression. But don't spend a lot of time on changing things here. We are still into discovery. If there are discrepancies between you, just note them. If you see things you want to change about yourself, it might be best if you just note that for future action, because we'll look at the Love and Logic tools-for-change later.

So, for the moment, don't get into long discussions about changing the attributes. Just take an honest look, firstly at how you see yourself, and secondly at how your partner sees you.

You will need at least half an hour of uninterrupted time to complete the following questionnaire. A middle-of-the-road answer is 3 and it should be obvious that this is a noncommittal answer, a wimp answer. Avoid being middle-of-the-road unless you are sure you want to be non-committal on a particular trait!

LOVE AND LOGIC ATTRIBUTE EVALUATION

© Foster & Hermie Cline

Love and Logic Attribute	I see myself (1–5)	I see my spouse (1–5)	My spouse will rate me (1–5)
Agressive			
Ambitious			
Assertive			
Cheerful			
Committed			
Contentious			
Courteous			
Creative and inventive			
Dependable			
Disciplined			
Easygoing			
Effective in action			
Empathetic			
Exercises judgment correctly			
Fair			
Forgiving			
Fun			
Giving			
Honest			
Independent			
Intelligent			
Laughs			
Logical			
Motivated			
Patient			
Persistent			
Polite			
Rational			
Responsible			
Self-confident			
Self-controlled			
Sharing			
Sharp-looking appropriately			
Straightforward			
Sympathetic			
Takes chances appropriately			
Thoughtful			
Trustworthy			

This chapter should have given you a fair amount of "grist for the mill," so to speak. Just don't grind each other up. Every couple has attributes and issues they see similarly, and those they disagree on. Join the human race. This has been a chapter of exploration, not a chapter on the tools and techniques of change. But hold on to your hat. That's coming up. And it is in the area of growth and change that committed couples have a distinct advantage. You are living with a person who can become, or perhaps is, a helpmate and soulmate.

The next chapter has to do with problem solving, compromising and accommodating each other in ways that will help you to at least come closer to being deliriously happy with each other.

CHAPTER

8

Action Plans and Problem Solving

What Happened to the Spark?

Awful as it sounds, even in the best of marriages, the person we romanced becomes the person we often criticize or hassle. How in the world does this happen?

The concept of romance is complicated. Even the dictionary appears to be a little uncertain. It says it is a love affair; idealized love; strong, short-lived enthusiasm; or to make love. Romance is more than simply making another person happy. Romance is really the wonder of surprise. As couples first get to know each other, their romance blooms easily because there is so much *to learn* about the other. Human beings love learning new things, and when the new thing is another person, *"Wow!"* Lights go off and bells ring.

Focus on the fact that wonder and surprise are a large part of romance. Without renewal, whether it is a person or a place, the wonder and surprise get thin. It's a case of stopping to admire the river valley before worrying about the mosquitoes. Or, to stay with the metaphor, we simply decide to camp among the beautiful alpine peaks and tundra before later realizing that four days is enough of this barren wasteland.

LOVE AND LOGIC TIP 34
Surprise and newness keep the spark alive.

Once the surprises stop, once we feel we've learned all we can, we start taking the object of our discovery for granted. A Las Vegas dealer once told us, "It doesn't take very long to lose feeling bedazzled by the dazzle."

Jay, a good friend, sitting with us in a beautiful pool, surrounded by marble fountains in a stunning Hawaiian hotel, laughed and half-jokingly said (though with some degree of amazement), "You know, I think it's only taken me about three days to get used to opulence! The towel heaters in our room could keep the towels a little warmer. I'll have to talk to management about that!"

As the newness wears off, humans start looking for things that could be changed. It occurs with spouses and houses. Don't we just love the house we buy? We say it's perfect; but before long, we realize the backyard "needs a patio" or the basement "really should be finished." It's as if we marry someone perfect so we can improve on them.

This drive for newness has led a few men in our couple groups to insist that their wives wear wigs or otherwise change their appearance prior to sex. Most of the wives were not enthusiastic about this suggestion. They figured that there must be a better way to keep romance alive. Enthusiastic or not, some wives acquiesced: "I'd rather be a fake blonde than find Al with a real one." This human drive for change can lead to men leaving a very lovely place or person. In many instances we've known people who discovered that moving on was not necessarily moving up. One man told us, "If I spent half as much energy on my first marriage as I've spent on this second one, I'd still be married to my first wife."

Let's just think about how one keeps any spark alive. If you just look at a spark and take it for granted, it isn't going to last long. To keep it alive it needs flowing, fresh oxygen and more material to burn. In our marriage the oxygen is our effort. The material to burn is the other's response to that effort and what we consciously put into the relationship. And all this has to be carried out around work, kids, shopping. It's a tall order to keep blowing on that spark! Take your eye off it, and it can disappear. In a lot of marriages, the spark was there, the fire was lit, and as time passes only the ashes of a passive congenial relationship remain. Pleasant but not hot.

Taking the other for granted shifts the focus off of doing things to primarily please the other into behaving as the other will tolerate. As a rude example, we usually don't crudely, noisily and easily pass gas around someone until we've lived with them for a while. (Isn't that sad but true!) And there is another issue that is related to our shifting toward what our spouse will tolerate. The sneaky flip side of positive attributes starts crawling out of our personalities. These shadow attributes may become more obvious as we relax around the other person and show "who we really are":

Persistence may shade into stubbornness.
An organized person may become fussy.
A relaxed person may become disorganized or sloppy.
A decisive person may become demanding.
Acceptable perfectionism may lead to procrastination.

Being married to a person does not imply ownership. Occasionally this happens after the wedding when a person feels entitled to control after those vows have been said. "Now Jack reminds me constantly that I *promised* to stick with him 'for better or worse.' He says it's *my problem* that I had no glimpse of his worst side." There are situations where people had no idea that there was quicksand in the meadow of flowers until deciding to lie down. Some spouses actually consider their mates a possession acquired on the day of their wedding vows. The following statement can be either healthy or very unhealthy depending upon how much possession underlies it: "You belong to me now! *My* house, *my* car and *my* spouse!" Although possession can play a role, the spark is often lost from lack of effort and lack of response to effort; we get too busy and our focus is fragmented.

Change itself can be hard. But the good thing about change is that it must be present for growth. Love it or hate it, there's no growth without change. The trick is how change and newness occur. Is it resolution or revolution, compromise or divorce? So, with the understanding that sparks must be attended to and that relationships *always* change, we are going to focus now on how couples thrive and manage that change to reach loving solutions.

Good Information Is the Foundation for Change

We are assuming that you have completed the evaluation exercises in Chapter 7 before proceeding further. Having done so, you will have gathered valuable data and insight about your marriage, maybe even more than you wanted to know! Now you will develop an action plan by which to handle the differences you found. Without a plan, things can get mired down in disagreements that go nowhere. Marriages are "made in heaven," but so are hurricanes and tornadoes. Just as cloudy weather can hide the sun, the occurrence of constant disagreements without compromises and solutions clouds the love you both felt when you married each other.

Reaching loving compromises and living with acceptable accommodations is what caring, lasting relationships are all about! Perhaps that doesn't sound very exciting on the surface, but then, it's not the surface that is usually important. And reaching those compromises, accommodations and solutions is part and parcel of what brings us close. Logic plays a role in tweaking those changes, which is why we call this *Love and Logic*. Marriages with love but little logic often fall into habitual conflict. You are about to learn to use Love and Logic problem-solving tools that will lead you to feel closer as you work things through.

Wise couples know they disagree. But they agree to have disagreements. And they agree on how to disagree. A wise spouse might say, "Marriage is a situation where I accommodate my honey's compromises!" Here is another paradox. The acceptance of disagreements allows us to relax enough to find accommodations that can lead us to both feel that we win. When we can't accept the other's viewpoint and we are so uptight and so set on winning, we both generally lose!

LOVE AND LOGIC TIP 35

Great marriages are a blend of essential
accommodations and vital compromises.

Three Areas for Problem Solving, Accommodation and Compromise

Every couple experiences problems within their marriage. These problems and differences can be broken down into three areas.

1. **Teamwork Issues:** These include problems that you both recognize are happening in the daily function of your marriage. These are issues that occur with every couple over schedules, priorities and

job descriptions. Talking over these issues ensures smooth *functioning* in your home. Helpmates talk easily about teamwork decisions.

2. **Recognized Issues:** These are those personal tasks for which each individual in the marriage is responsible. Issues in this category involve following through on personal commitments, time issues, problems in being overly defensive, taking things too personally ... the list could go on and on, of course. We call these problems "Sliver in the Finger" issues. A sliver in the finger is annoying to the owner of that finger. And both can see it. Probably anyone can see it! It's an issue that the owner of the finger has to deal with or ignore. Slivers such as smoking may not be easily dealt with. On these issues, a person might say to his or her spouse that he or she has a problem and wants to change it. For example, "I have a need to tone down my public political rants." These personal issues are perfect ones to solve within a helpmate relationship.

3. **Hidden Issues:** These are individual issues that are seen by one partner, but not the other. Many character traits are issues that we, ourselves, have trouble seeing. And even when we see them, we may not want to change them, or we feel hopeless about changing them. We call these "Egg on the Face" issues. They are harder to deal with and ideally are solved within a soulmate relationship.

Let's look at each of these areas in more detail:

Teamwork Issues

LOVE AND LOGIC TIP 36
A marriage workshop may be successful simply because couples take the time and energy to set priorities and work through teamwork issues.

Mutually recognized problems need to be managed for your marriage to function smoothly. Again, such problems require attentive communication, organization and an action plan or you won't find solutions. Relatively speaking, this category usually has the easiest problems to solve. Issues in this category might be:

Who does what chore within our couple relationship.

Let's make more time for each other.

Let's get a handle on financial matters.

Let's curb our eating out.

Let's plan more time with the family.

Let's make time for individual needs.

Let's meet new friends.

Accommodations and compromises will need to be reached. How do we make more time for each other? *How do we set our priorities as a couple?* The three main reasons for conflict in this area are:

1. Severe couple control battles (which are almost always the product of personal issues).
2. Poor communication skills.
3. Most frequently, simply not taking time to set priorities or talk about how the week or day needs to be planned.

Recognized Issues

Problems falling into the recognized or "Sliver in the Finger" category are those that are mutually recognized and for which the owner of the problem either wants to solve the issue or can be talked into committing to solve it. There are advantages and dangers to both individuals being involved in the plan to solve the problem. The advantages are many: the helpmates often become closer, communication is clarified, mutual goals are discussed and loving feelings occur with the acceptance, assistance and compromises that are often part and parcel of the solution. The danger is that the partner becomes more invested, insistent and controlling about removing the sliver than the individual who has it stuck in the finger. Personal resolve and self-discipline are key for both partners.

LOVE AND LOGIC TIP 37
Sliver in the Finger
One individual owns and recognizes the problem. The helpmate, when requested, assists in the plan for solving it.

Issues that often fall in the "Sliver in the Finger" category might be:

I'd like to lose weight.

I'd like to be more organized.

I'd like to spend more time with my spouse.

I'd like to exercise more.

I'd like to get a grip on my spending

Hidden Issues

Hidden or "Egg on the Face" issues are tricky. What we recognize in another is influenced by what we, ourselves, are prone to see. Pots tend to call kettles black. Women who grow up with abusive men may see a raised voice as verbal abuse. Men dominated by their mother confuse their wife's assertiveness with aggressiveness. If there are to be changes in this area, "Egg on the Face" issues require couples to possess tact, trust, thoughtfulness and the ability for self-examination. That's a tall order. Lots of relationships simply don't have all four. This is an area requiring soulmate activity if solutions are to be reached. Certainly, helping a partner deal with individual issues is what being a helpmate and soulmate is all about. However, it's the proper handling of soulmate issues that leads couples to develop a rewarding and fulfilling relationship. This is the area of real personality and character growth. Tact and thoughtfulness are required because one partner may have a hard time recognizing specific negative character traits. Often these character traits are not "solved" but worked around. Compromise and accommodation work best in these areas. However, if one partner accommodates to the other's problem, of course that accommodating person may grow (or be stunted, as the case may be), but the one with the issue may not grow at all.

Typical "Egg on the Face" issues that might be recognized by a spouse:

Being defensive
Telling inappropriate jokes
Acting inappropriately in public
Flirting
Acting crudely
Substance abuse
Not taking care of health issues
Losing faith in him- or herself
Berating the children
Whining
Being unaffectionate

Regardless of the perceived problem, as we noted, the recognition of personality and character problems is oftentimes dependent upon the partner:

Troy occasionally does not pick up after himself. He may leave his jacket and coat in the living room, his cap hooked on a chair in the dining room. Mary doesn't like living with a "slob." What is the problem? Who owns it? Troy says, "Hey, it's my house. I'm not a neatnik. Give me a break. Okay, okay, it's my fault. I married an obsessive-compulsive." He really doesn't see his behavior as a problem. Troy thinks Mary has a problem.

Regardless of who has the problem, this couple may be a little short on the big four: tact, trust, thoughtfulness and self-examination. A smattering of tenderness might lacking too. As a matter of fact, if all four were present there might not even be a need to "solve the problem."

"Egg on the Face" problems have many facets. For one thing, when one or the other does not recognize that there is a problem, it makes for a lot of silent stewing. When Troy does not pick up after himself and doesn't even want to talk about it, Mary thinks long and hard about the reasons:

He's stressed out.
His personality traits make him a natural born slob.
He is passive/aggressive and wants to make me work harder.
Okay, he's thoughtful, just super-absentminded.

Mary also stews silently about the choices she has in handling what she sees as Troy's problem. She ruminates on ways to:

Pick up after him, pleasantly.
Pick up after him while complaining every step of the way.
Ask him to pick up after himself.
Demand that he pick up after himself.
Content herself with telling others, in public, what a slob she married.

Love and Logic Action Planning

Stewing about why a person acts the way he or she does certainly may make life less boring and it certainly fills the time void, but it is usually irrelevant to problem solving. Wondering what we can do to take care of ourselves is generally more productive. Taking good care of ourselves may mean engaging our spouse in a discussion about the issue and developing an action plan.

The *Love and Logic Action Plan* is designed to help couples solve problems and reach mutually beneficial accommodations and compromises. The five components of an action plan are:

1. A recognition of the problem.
2. A willingness to communicate about the problem.
3. A willingness to work together to develop solutions.
4. Discipline on both sides to carry out the plan to reach the solution.
5. Follow-up and revisitation of the issue periodically.

Discussing the Action Plan

"Egg on the Face" issues really do require a partnership. Somehow, a mate must encourage discussion about personal issues that his or her partner might rather not hear. A spouse who presents it with thoughtful love and tact can encourage problem solving. Even then a person might be defensive. Don't we all know the flavors of denial:

"I don't know where you got *that* idea!"
"Why are you making this up?"
"You can't really believe what you're saying!"
"Well, nobody else sees it that way!"
"You can be unhappy with it, but I'm not!"
"Do you have a headache? Are you feeling okay?"

There will be no discussion and solving of these issues unless we are around a spouse whom we trust and with whom we can communicate well. When couples manage to work through "Egg on the Face" issues in a way that both grow, we call this kind of relationship a "soulmate relationship."

Nelson was a successful contractor. At least, he looked successful. But he borrowed money from Peter to pay Paul. And the further he got himself into debt, the more secretively he behaved and the more ashamed he felt. Finally, as it always does, all of his scheming came crashing down when Cindy opened an unpaid bill. Nelson knew it would be the end of his marriage. Cindy would be furious. She had every right to be.

Commenting on our porch a year later, Nelson said, "But I'll say this for her, I couldn't have a better accountant. She's an expert financial planner. I make the money, and she has really kept me on track. I can understand the pretty graphs she makes, but I'm not good with the green stuff. And I like it that way. I had been so insistent on handling the family finances! As I look back on it, it must have been some sort of death wish. I only wish that I could have admitted years ago that handling money was a problem for me, and then let her be my accountant. Instead of leaving me, she helped us get through it together." Cindy snuggles in and laughs, "Yeah, now I can do no wrong, and I'm going to collect, buddy, remember that!" One can only guess what that might be. But do you know what? They're soulmates and they'll get through it!

The Secret of Love and Logic Problem Solving

We've implied it, but now we'll say it outright: *The only way you can help another person with their problem is their way!*

The whole secret of developing a helpmate and soulmate relationship is having a spoken or unspoken contract. No one appreciates unasked-for advice or suggestions about their own character or functioning.

A wife is dressing for a party. She asks, "Honey, do you think this dress looks good on me?" He says quite honestly, "No, it makes you look fat." She says, "Why in the world would say something like that to me?" He says, "Golly, you asked, didn't you? What do you want me to do, lie?"

He *should* have responded to her question by responding, "Sorry, Dear. There was a was better way to handle that, right?" And then she would say, "Yeah, like saying ... 'Maybe the green outfit would be more slimming.' I think I could handle that." And he should say, "Good idea" not "I didn't know you had a green outfit."

The secret is finding out from our loved ones what *they* see as a problem, and then asking *them* how it might be helpful for us to respond.

As months pass, my weight rheostat keeps being reset somehow. Slowly the girth seems to flow outward. Hermie can help me develop a little self-control around eating. But it probably wouldn't be helpful if she commented, "Honey, you remind me of a moving oil barrel" or "Any more weight and we'll need floor supports." Around some things, my sense of humor is somehow lacking. But Hermie is a very wise wife. After I comment on my problems, she says, *"Is there anything I could say that you think would be helpful?"* I say, "I think if you asked, 'Do you really want that second helping?' it would probably be as helpful as anything else. Then I have the option of saying yes or no. Then I would appreciate your not giving me that torqued-out look if I say I really do want it."

Hermie agreed, with a provision: "Let's give it a shot. But if you constantly and consistently say, 'Yeah, I want that second helping,' I will probably back off the question."

As I sit writing this sentence, I've lost forty pounds. And I'm trying to catch that little elf that adjusts the rheostat.

For both "Sliver in the Finger" and "Egg on the Face" issues, here are the Love and Logic problem-solving steps:

1. I decide I *want* to change.
2. I figure out how my helpmate can be useful.
3. I ask for my spouse's help, with the understanding he or she can respond with a yes or no.
4. The issue is revisited after it has had some time to show failure or success. If it is working, then keep going. If it isn't, don't keep turning the ignition key harder because the car won't start.

THE HELPMATE EXPERIENCE

Handling "Sliver in the Finger" Issues

As you gathered information about your relationship from the *Love and Logic Experiences* in the last chapter, you probably found things that you wish were different. If you didn't find anything at all that you wish were different, you are either newly married, separated or one of you is dead! All of the issues that we might want changed can be divided into the three major groups that we have discussed. They are *my* problems, *your* problems and *our teamwork* problems (and many of them can overlap). As we've shown, we can further divide individual issues into things we can see ("Sliver in the Finger") or can't or don't want to recognize ("Egg on the Face"). In this exercise we are going to look at helpmate issues. It will take about thirty minutes.

Look at the results from your *Love and Logic Couples Evaluation* from Chapter 7. If for some reason you do not have those responses handy, simply follow the directions below and come up with new, "pristine" information.

On a separate piece of paper write a list of:

1. Three things that you can do together to improve your relationship. These are teamwork issues.
2. Three things your spouse sees that you can do to improve your relationship. (This can be the same as those listed for step 1 above, but not necessarily. Be as thorough as you can be.)
3. Three things you see that your spouse can do to improve your relationship.

Now choose one or two issues about yourself that you think you would like to change. Practice the five steps of contracting for helpmate change:

1. "Honey, I have a problem I would like you to help me with. Can we discuss it? Is this a good time?"
2. "Yes."
3. "When I _____, I would like you to notice it by saying or responding with _____. Can you do that?"
4. "Sure."
5. "Thanks."

Notice that the initiating partner has to come up with his or her own problem and be willing or motivated to change it. Further, the owner of the problem must come up with the method and statements that the spouse might use to help.

Play with this outside the exercise. Practice it. You will begin to recognize other things you wish were different for yourself, and as you and your partner play with these issues, your appreciation for each other will grow.

Needless to say, there are numerous and unusual variations on the help-mate responses. The steps do not need to be set in concrete or formalized in any way. Partners help each other with loving, humorous comments that take the bite out of critical observations every time. To an outsider these interrelational quips might sound sarcastic, but when said with love, in homes where there is a great deal of trust, such comments can be quite helpful.

When my son went off to college, he said, "Dad, you should exercise. Sit-ups would help. But don't strain yourself, do two!"

 View "Your Help Mate Relationship" on the DVD. Watching Rob and Amy, notice how affection, tenderness and understanding are essential when working through these issues.

THE SOULMATE EXPERIENCE

Handling "Egg on the Face" Issues

Finally, we are dealing with the most difficult issues. The things partners see in each other, not recognized by the self. Such issues must, with tact, be brought up by the partner for possible recognition and resolution.

First, on a piece of paper write down two traits that you feel you have worked around, or ignored with your spouse. These can be areas where you have willingly compromised or accommodated, but other options would be nice. Second, ask your spouse if he or she sees the issue and would like to discuss it.

Give yourselves thirty minutes. That's usually enough time in one sitting on one item that could be a "hot-button" issue. If you run a perceptual check ("How do you think we are doing?") and you both feel good about your discussion, you can continue the discussion now or later.

Outside of this *Love and Logic Experience,* the usual way of approaching these issues would be to pick a microsecond you are both in a good mood and bring up the issue gently, tenderly, with great love: "Honey, I'd like to talk to you about something you do that you may not see and that I wish were different. Is this a good time?" If the answer is yes, then pick a time or place. Ideally a nice restaurant that you both enjoy. The cozier the better. If the answer is no, try bringing it up once more. If the answer is always no, then accommodate, compromise or find outside help.

Truthfully, issues that are hidden from self-observation are often very ingrained or otherwise very hard to change. Truly happy couples often don't try to "fix" or "solve" "Egg on the Face" traits, but often compromise or work around them. Keep in mind that however you handle it, accommodation can occasionally slide into codependency or enabling.

LOVE AND LOGIC TIP 38

Accommodation, in extreme, may inexorably lead to enabling or codependency.

If you can't make headway or discuss helpmate and soulmate issues, then you will have to accept your spouse's behaviors or insist on working through them with counseling. It's fortunate when a couple can actually function happily on a soulmate level and help each other grow.

Marriage Paths Summary

The diagram below gives an overview of the paths a marriage may take as couples interact. They may accommodate, compromise and/or help each other grow. The diagram is really a summary of this chapter. You may take one road on some issues, and another road on others. Look at it together. What path are you both most comfortable with?

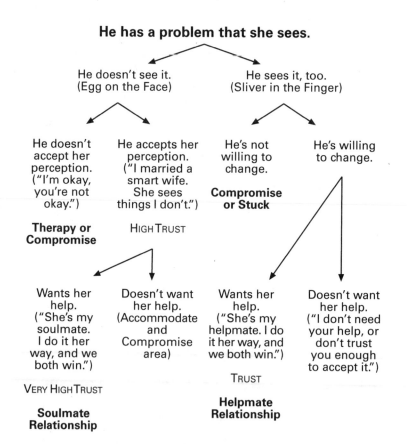

He has a problem that she sees.

He doesn't see it.
(Egg on the Face)

He sees it, too.
(Sliver in the Finger)

He doesn't accept her perception.
("I'm okay, you're not okay.")

Therapy or Compromise

He accepts her perception.
("I married a smart wife. She sees things I don't.")

HIGH TRUST

He's not willing to change.

Compromise or Stuck

He's willing to change.

Wants her help.
("She's my soulmate. I do it her way, and we both win.")

VERY HIGH TRUST

Soulmate Relationship

Doesn't want her help.
(Accommodate and Compromise area)

Wants her help.
("She's my helpmate. I do it her way, and we both win.")

TRUST

Helpmate Relationship

Doesn't want her help.
("I don't need your help, or don't trust you enough to accept it.")

In this chapter we have looked at some issues that could be sensitive and difficult. But they are also the issues that will bring you much closer when you successfully deal with them using good communication skills, affection and thoughtful accommodation.

CHAPTER

9

Life Scripts:
Messages from Childhood

❧

ONE WAY OR ANOTHER, we deserve each other. Our personalities, our pasts, our characters and our culture all play a role in those we find attractive. This is a chapter of discovery about the nuances of "fit." Sure, some folks in the heat of passion find the nearest Justice of the Peace and get hitched. But that's not as common as it used to be. For better or for worse, many folks these days live together to find out if they fit. The individuals forming a couple have a *touching* relationship. They are not two peas in a pod. Those two little peas don't touch, at least not much. Two spheres certainly can't curl around each other. Only a round hole would fit a pea. Things that are exactly the same just don't fit. That's why we generally don't choose someone just like ourselves to marry. Couples fit. Couples are complementary. Couples are more like the "wind beneath my wings" metaphor or more like the jeans and the young girls who struggle to pour themselves into those jeans. You get the point. Individuals in a

couple relationship fit. And whether or not the fit is there in the beginning, it doesn't take long for the fit to develop when people interact.

When Hermie and I first married, she really didn't know that she
was marrying one of the world's most absentminded young men.
When I would misplace my keys, for instance, I could ask, "Honey,
have you seen my keys?" Like the wonderful newlywed sweetheart
she was, she would help me look. My unconscious self somehow
always allowed her, after a short search, to find the keys, whereupon she would give the exultant, "Here they are!" and I would
say, "Thank *you, Honey.*"

Through those first months I unconsciously trained her to keep
track of my stuff. I didn't do it on purpose. Inside the first six
months of marriage, I could ask, "Honey, have you seen my keys?"
Her sweet reply was usually, "I think I saw 'em on the back of the
dresser," or something similar. Within a year, I only had to look
puzzled and slightly lost before leaving for the office. She would
say, without hesitation, "*Dresser!*" Without even trying to, I had
transformed my wife into an object-oriented real-time database.
She knew where every item that could be carried or misplaced was
located. So that was good. She developed more than enough memory for both of us.

The fit in marriage can be seen everywhere. Jack Sprat can eat no fat,
his wife can eat no lean. Jack and his wife fit; that is, they weigh together
about what two ordinary people should. In other words, a heel might only
be happy with a doormat. An obsessive, compulsive person often marries
someone pretty loose, maybe even slightly sloppy. Often, obsessive people
tend to be angry people. If there is no one around to project anger onto,
they can give themselves a pretty hard time. So it's good to have a spouse

to project all that anger onto when something looks out of place. Two obsessives, of course, drive each other crazy! Like two peas in a pod, they might be together for a while, but they wouldn't fit.

In high school, you will often see the kids who are happy with their parents hooking up with other kids who are happy with their parents because happy fits happy. People for whom loving another comes easily usually marry others who easily love others. We deserve each other!

We passed a matronly woman the other day while shopping at a wholesale warehouse. She had the statement "A husband is the kid who never grows up and won't move out" emblazoned on a T-shirt that stretched across bouncing bounteous bosoms. Hermie and I laughed silently about the fit. (Not the shirt, the couple.)

Even if such a statement were true, why brag about it?! Do you want everyone to know you chose a boob for a husband? And if it's not true, why buy the shirt? To our perception, this lady was evidently happy in her role as queen of the palace. And to whom must such a person be married? Sure enough, shuffling along behind the walking billboard came the lost child of a husband who would have been swallowed alive wearing her shirt. He followed like a footman, putting the food she pointed out into the cart.

Few husbands would appreciate being treated like this, or even be willing to put up with it. (What woman would be overjoyed following behind a husband whose shirt proclaimed "My wife is such a ditz!") If for some reason a wife or husband insisted on wearing one of these negative broadband broadcasts, the spouse might understandably say, "If you're going to wear that shirt, I'll just stay home because I don't want to be seen with you." But of course a person who would wear the shirt would never marry such an assertive spouse. (Again, notice that assertive people say where *they* stand, not what the *other person* has to do!)

You've learned about paraphrasing and studied the Love and Logic communication tools. They're important because without them, no relationship can happily survive. If you can't talk, you can't study or understand your walk. Communication, like the waves on the ocean, simply provides a smoother environment from which to launch the bathysphere to study the more interesting currents below. The deeper currents of your individual personalities beckon you to discover insights that will help you grow through mutual understanding. Since you have gone over the communication tools and used them in relating around the evaluation issues, we think you are ready to plumb the interesting depths of personality development. These "beneath the surface" issues may flow through many aspects of your relationship. They influence the way you make decisions about purchases, the way you show love and your acceptance levels.

Many parents rightly worry that their children are not choosing correctly. The earlier puppy love of falling head over heals for anyone, and screaming unendingly at any rock star, hopefully gives way to more thoughtful appraisals of specific individuals. It's a stage-specific process. Teens are figuring out who they want to be with. Generally speaking, in high school, teens who get along well with their parents choose boyfriends or girlfriends who also get along well with their parents. Adolescents with difficult backgrounds are attracted to other children with difficult backgrounds. Boys who have a great relationship with their moms generally choose girls who love their dads.

And if their home environments are loving, the old song stanza "I want a girl just like the girl who married dear old dad" both is true and generally comes true.

LOVE AND LOGIC TIP 39

The unrecognized atmosphere of our
childhood home may secretly spoil or
enhance our marriage environment.

The emotions, behaviors, relationships and responses in childhood color our vision. If we grew up with anger, we tend to be oversensitive to another's anger and tend to either have a very short fuse or hide our own anger. If we grew up in a loving home, loving responses come naturally. If we grew up in a home where emotional displays were frequent and accepted, then we generally show emotion easily. If our parents were obsessive about neatness, we tend toward excessive neatness or strongly reject neatness. The road to Rome and the road away from Rome are the very same road. Therefore, women who either obsessively clean their home because their mother is coming, or obsessively leave it a mess, are both controlled by childhood emotions promoted by their mothers.

Janet thinks Paul is the easiest man in the world to cook for. He'll eat leftovers ... anything ... and he's thankful for them. "I never have to hassle my head about cooking to please him. He's a working wife's dream!"

Paul laughs in response. "When I went off to the Army after high school and all the other grunts were complaining about army food, I thought I was in hog heaven. Army food was the best! See, my mom hated to cook. And smell and taste proved it! My brother and I used to plead for Swanson's pot pies. 'Please Mom, please Mom, don't cook! Can't we have fried Spam?' There weren't many kids in our neighborhood who wanted to hop right on over and have the boiled tongue, sweet breads and tripe my mom cooked! But when you combine a mom with a farm childhood with a woman who doesn't like to cook anyway, you raise a couple of kids who aren't too fussy about food!"

There are all sorts of pleasant or outright enjoyable outcomes from strange behaviors learned in childhood. When I first married Hermie, I was somewhat surprised at the excitement, resolve and outright pleasure she took in untying knots. She was actually pleased when there were knots in my shoelaces that she could untie. Strange! She explained that she had two older brothers who were the "cowboys" during her childhood. She was the "Indian" they left hog-tied on the ground or strapped to a tree. They'd tie her up and literally run off, leaving her there for hours. From that, she took real pride in being able to free herself by outwitting their knot-tying. Sometimes it took her hours to get free. Even as we age, my wife still enjoys the challenge of my knotty laces.

Habitual patterns of "preferred" interaction with others have been called *Life Scripts*. Of course, *Life Scripts* written in childhood days often play a deeper role than how we respond to food and knots. They may have to do with a fear of abandonment or may play a role in the constant fear of those who anticipate things will work out poorly. Similarly, childhood education in interpersonal dynamics also plays a role in the optimism of those who somehow expect things to go well almost all the time.

When our vision is colored by difficult or unresponsive childhoods, we often can't see the true tint of our own emotion or the emotions of those around us. When I go skiing, I wear orange ski goggles. Soon after putting them on, the outside world looks natural enough to me. My brain compensates to the tint of my lenses. Intellectually, I know I am seeing a different color spectrum than companions who wear gray or silvered goggles. But it usually doesn't come up and is of little consequence, until we talk specifically about a particular coat worn by another skier:

"Hey, look at that red coat! Isn't it pretty?"
"What red coat? I don't see any red coat."
"That one, right there that the brunette is wearing."
"You mean that off-white coat? What's so pretty about that?"

This is analogous to a conversation Rick and Rachael might have wearing their different childhood goggles:

"You don't have to get so angry with me."

"I'm not angry at you."

"Well you sound angry."

"I just don't know where you get that. Sure, I'm feeling a little frustrated right now, but I'm not sounding angry at you."

Using the ski-goggle example, when wearing orange lenses I can't tell a red ski jacket from a white one. Plus, I confuse blue and black. If my friend is wearing blue sunglasses, he confuses blue with white, and red with black. *We need each other to provide perceptual checks to understand the truth of things.*

Couples need each other for the same reason: Each of us serves the other as a perceptual check on the reality of things. And that perceptual check is most useful when we perceive, experience or express emotions. As time passes in marriage, individuals come to have an increased appreciation (or an increased dismay) that they and their honey see things differently based on a childhood education long ago and largely forgotten.

In our couple relationships we often marry individuals who see things differently. We marry people who are complementary to us. In analogy, a person who wears red goggles from childhood is likely to be attracted to a person who wears blue sunglasses. *Together their soulmate trip is to figure out how things "really are."* Boys who have problems with their mothers often marry girls who have problems with their fathers.

Throughout our marriage, there have been times that Hermie and I have seen things very differently. And at times she says, "Foster, trust me on this. You just aren't seeing it correctly." When we were first married, sad to say, I more often thought, "Poor lass, she has no idea how wrong she is." As the years have passed, I'm more likely to say, "Well, I married her because she is smart and perceptive, so listen up, buddy."

LOVE AND LOGIC TIP 40
How many of us have the trust to believe things are the way our spouse perceives them, not the way we see them?

Common Confusions Left Over from Childhood

Hermie and I have found that there tend to be eight common confusions shared by many couples. These confusions muddy the waters of marital clarity. They equally muddy the waters of successful parenting and, in fact, all leadership effectiveness. The eight confusions are related. A person who has one of them will usually have several, because both the concepts themselves and their genesis in childhood are related. Often, the individuals who have the most problem with these common confusions come from difficult, disturbed and/or dysfunctional backgrounds. Of course, any of us can mix up empathy and sympathy, approval and acceptance, at times. But most couples don't have major problems with these confusions unless a difficult history lurks in the background.

THE EIGHT COMMON CONFUSIONS

Selfish	Self-Care
Aggressive	Assertive
Punitive	Cosequential
Approving	Accepting
Bribe	Reward
Threat	Facts
Empathy	Sympathy
Being Mean	Meaning Business

Selfish – Self-Care

The first principle of Love and Logic is to take good care of yourself so that you can set the model for others. The major message of ALANON and all self-help groups is to back off attempting to control others and instead make sure you treat yourself right. It is never selfish to take good care of yourself. Ultimately everyone around you wins, too. Remember, we wrote earlier that life must be a win/win or ultimately lose/lose position. People who take good care of themselves set the model for all those around them to act like winners too. Parents who model self-care and don't let their children push them around or be disrespectful to them are much more likely to raise children immune to peer pressure. Self-care is the foundation of the Golden Rule.

Aggressive – Assertive

An assertive person says, "This is where I stand." An aggressive person says, "This is where you need to go"; or its more common variation, "What you need to do is ..."

In our marriages, when one individual is not properly assertive, it encourages the other to become increasingly more aggressive, demanding and controlling. Some folks learn in childhood that they just don't count. They grow up in environments where other people always get their way. If it's a man, he easily confuses his wife's assertiveness with her being overly demanding. When she says, "John, I need you to do this for me," he responds, "Don't tell me what to do!" People who are not assertive are camels. They carry a lot of straws while quietly struggling. Finally, it's the last straw. By then they have held in their feelings so long that they erupt. It takes such a pressure buildup for them to say anything that when it does blow, there's camel droppings everywhere! "Hey, it's not fair for you to load all those straws on me! You have no regard for my back! What do you think I am, some sort of beast of burden?!!!" What the person should have said, firmly, meaning business without being mean, 10,456 straws ago is, "I'm unwilling to carry any more of your load." And then give choices: "Would you like to find another camel, carry more of it yourself or just leave that baggage behind?"

Punitive – Consequential

People who have grown up with either rescuing parents or abusive parents feel "it's just not fair" when they have to actually cope with the negative consequences of their own actions.

Molly grew up with folks who rescued her. They even paid for college courses, which she cut and flunked. During her college years they paid bills she recklessly accumulated. Soon after her marriage to Rick, it was obvious Molly couldn't handle money. So, together they made a budget. Molly did not stay within her budget for personal and discretionary items. She felt Rick was absolutely unfair when he wouldn't take money from other areas to make up for her deficit spending. Unconsciously, Molly believed, "My mommy only allowed me to suffer if she was punishing me. So Rick must be punishing me." With the patience of Job, Rick attempted to clarify: "I'm not punishing you, Honey, but you made these commitments, and you'll have to live within them. If you overspent this month, it comes out of your budget for next month."

"You're being mean" (i.e., punitive) is the cry of the child whose parents don't take them to school when he or she is late, don't make a special trip to bring something to school that he or she forgot, etc. Some adults just feel the whole world is against them when the bill collector knocks at the door after they have overspent.

In the case of spouses who grew up with abusive parents, all pain suffered in their childhoods was because of *unjustified* punishment. For these folks, any discomfort that can occur while coping with consequences is also seen as unjustified.

Approving – Accepting

Acceptance of a spouse's view or behavior is not the same thing as approving of their view or behavior. Wise individuals accept what they cannot change. They may thoughtfully let others know whether or not they approve.

LOVE AND LOGIC TIP 41

Keep the lines of communication open: Acceptance means listening with caring to things you'd rather not hear.

Laurie said, "Ron forgot I planned to use the truck yesterday morning. He took it and I needed it for the garden show. I just won't accept his forgetting like that." We say, "Wait a minute, Laurie. It's already happened! What you mean is you don't approve of it. But you'd better, for your own peace of mind, accept it." Most faith-filled adults see God as *accepting* of their prayers. How many prayers reach his heavenly ears and lead him to respond, "What a nice little hymn of praise—I haven't heard that one before" or "What a nice and thoughtfully phrased request." The Catholic Confessional is the perfect example of a place where people can go and feel accepted, and yet know there is disapproval of their thoughts or actions. And the lines of communication are kept open.

Bribe – Reward

Some spouses suffered angry parent-child interactions, growing up in homes where parents seldom did things for the children because they *wanted* to. More often, they did things with and for the children because it was their *duty* or they felt they *had* to. Such people confuse rewards and bribes, especially when it has to do with the children. If the adults themselves get a bonus or raise, they are not as likely to see it as a bribe as they may when paying their children for a job especially well done.

This bribe/reward confusion more often comes up in parenting disputes—around giving children money for grades, for instance. Giving children money may be both a reward and a bribe. But those who give rewards do so because it makes them happy. A bribe is delivered without joy because the giver feels cornered into supplying it.

Threat – Facts

Threats are generally the result of fear, and are most often said with anger. Threats are often spewed out from a frustrated position, which in itself says the person has no control of the situation. Donna often said, "If this continues, I'm going to divorce you." James never paid attention to her because she always shouted it in a rage. He knew it was "just Donna's monthly threat routine." He never changed the behavior that so understandably enraged his wife. Following a round of therapy, Donna said quietly one day, "James, I've given the issue a lot of thought. And I think perhaps it would be best if we separated." Donna, telling of this in a group, while James nods agreeably, says, "Wow. Did his ears ever prick up. He knew I meant it." James hugs her and says, "It was that sprinkling of sorrow that you threw in there. I was used to the threats said with anger. They never meant a thing."

Empathy – Sympathy

There is a place for both sympathy and empathy in marriage. But there is a difference. Sympathy says, "Your sorrow makes me feel bad too." Empathy says, "I can understand how you are feeling." When people cause themselves trouble and consequences, empathy is called for: "Golly, what a mess you have made for yourself. I understand how upset you must be." Sympathy is called for when something happens beyond a person's control and he or she is feeling bereaved: "I share in your loss of your mother. She was a good friend to us all." Both sympathy and empathy are "okay emotions." The fly in the ointment occurs because sympathy is sometimes dysfunctionally present in codependent relationships in which a spouse may be manipulated into sharing pain because of the nonsense the other has caused him- or herself. When people cause themselves problems, it is better to be empathetic than sympathetic. Great therapists are always empathetic. Too much sympathy from a therapist would actually be dismaying. He would not be setting the example of taking good care of himself. Can you imagine a therapist bursting into tears and saying to a client through his sobs, "That's the saddest divorce story I've ever heard. I'm really shaken up by it!"

Being Mean – Meaning Business

Again, this problem is sometimes seen around parenting issues. Some parents shout at their children, "Now I mean business!" These poor folks are saying, in effect, "I don't mean business unless I'm noisy." Few effective individuals show their leadership by being mean or noisy. Most of our great leaders have been quietly effective. And although not noisy, mean or threatening, there is no doubt they mean business.

How Life Scripts Interact: Summary Example

Jack, whose mother was often controlling and demanding, married Janette, whose father was generally irresponsible and an alcoholic. Jack was very sensitive to being "mothered" or being "controlled." Janette grew up thinking, "If things aren't quite right, I need to do more or act better." When this couple married, it was a perfect fit. And that sort of fit could easily result in either divorce or the bliss of a growing soulmate relationship. Divorce could have occurred because Jack and Janette outright abraded each other. Each poured salt into their spouse's wounds of childhood. Happily, they attended a weekend retreat.

If the fit of a couple relationship is to continue while one person changes, the other must make a congruent change. Jack and Janette accomplished this. Everyone can. But *only if you help each other out within a trusting relationship*. And whether or not a soulmate relationship becomes sublime or the pain results in divorce, there will always be a unique and bumpy road to follow. Jack and Janette had a lot of surface issues that they fought around prior to the workshop. But all those surface issues were pushed along by their hidden childhood scripts. Let's look at the situation in a diagram:

LIFE SCRIPTS INTERACT

Janette grew up with an irresponsible and alcoholic father. ("Only if I'm good enough, and do enough, will things turn out okay.")

Jack grew up with a demanding and controlling mother. ("Nothing I do is good enough.")

Ultimately, men will disappoint you.

Ultimately, women will control you.

I have to do everything.

You are never satisfied.

You are so irresponsible!

You are on my case about every little thing!

Why are you always leaving me?

I feel like I've got to get away.

You need to help me more.

You are too much of a perfectionist!

You drink too much.

A few beers on the weekend? A glass of wine perhaps in the evening?! You drive me to drink!

As shown in this diagram, each person had their own view of the relationship:

JACK

Jack saw Janette as "always trying to be in charge."

He hated it when Janette "ordered me around."

He was angry when she tried to control the money.

He was tired of her harping about his yearly hunting trips with old friends.

JANETTE

Janette saw Jack as spending too freely on incidentals and not
  planning for the future.

She was resentful when he forgot important dates, forgot to take
  out the trash and put off fixing things around the house.

She really hated his "going off all the time, wasting time with
  his duck-hunting buddies."

The major messages going back and forth between Jack and Janette might
be summarized as:

Janette to Jack: "Start acting responsible!"

Jack to Janette: "Would you please relax?!!!"

Underneath, both were more insecure about the other than was warranted. It was an insecurity driven by things long ago, unseen and unrecognized. And that problem had escalated into a vicious cycle by the time
of the workshop.

Hermie and I ran into Jack and Janette in a shopping mall six
months later and sat down and had coffee with them. Janette was

downright enthusiastic about the changes she had made for herself and within the couple relationship. "It was so hard, but it was basically simple. I started this way: Every time I started to feel like being on Jack's case, I would ask myself, 'If Jack were my father, would I be saying this to my dad?' Yep. Almost every time! What a wake-up call! First of all, I decided, instead of making all these internal statements, like, 'Jack, you are so irresponsible,' I started to ask questions or just give him the benefit of the doubt. Like, I might say, 'Honey (and boy, did the terms of endearment help), do you feel okay about fixing the screen on the slider this weekend?' And I'll tell you what was the hardest. When Jack felt I was into my "routine," I asked him to say, 'Honey, just relax. I'll handle it. I'm not your dad.' He didn't have to say it that often, 'cause I really hated hearing it. But it helped.

Jack piped up and said, "I realized that nothing I ever did was good enough for my mom. She just couldn't be satisfied. So when Janette would ask me to do something, I really did hear all requests as a command that could never be happily fulfilled. And I started saying to myself, 'This is a request I *can* do. I can please this woman. This is not my mom.' And I'd say to her, 'Honey, will this make you happy?' and she'd say, 'Sure.' And then I'd do it. And she absolutely was happy!"

Janette noted, "It was another wake-up call to realize after our couples weekend that it really was an internal uphill swim to say, 'Jack, thanks so much. You make me so happy.' I realized that it was darn hard to express pleasure seeing what the main man in my life accomplished. There was no pleasure with the main man in my childhood, and my script was to have no real pleasure with my man now."

If Jack and Janette could recognize their pattern, where it came from, and work together in a soulmate relationship to change things, you can too.

THE CHILDHOOD MATRIX

Love and Logic
Experience

The *Childhood Matrix* will provide you with an eye-opening experience. Let's look at what the matrix is all about. It provides an overview of the forest of our relationship. The trees of our relationship are the day-to-day things that we might discuss, argue over or resolve. The forest is the messages and experiences that flowed through our childhoods. Childhood experiences mainly affect those with whom we are intimate. Childhood experiences with our parents, brothers and sisters may play less of a role in how we relate to neighbors or peers at work. To give this exercise its due, you should plan on taking about twenty or thirty minutes of thoughtful cogitation to fill out the diagram and then spend about an hour together to discover things about yourself and your spouse. Like all the exercises in this book, it could be rushed. But don't do that. This one is to be *savored*.

One of the things you will be asked about (on the lower left) is your favorite story, movie or television program. It is not always only the protagonist or hero who is totally relevant. We remember one lady who read *Cinderella* over and over again. Someone in the group congratulated her on heading toward princesshood, whereupon she burst into tears and said, "No, no, I'm the wicked stepsister." Another lady recalled watching the old show *Howdy Doody*. (The name of the show will leave all of you younger folks clueless, but that's not important.) The point is, there was a "Peanut Gallery" of onlookers to the show. And the participant, with sudden, horrified insight, said, "I'm not Howdy Doody, I'm a member of the Peanut Gallery. All of my life I've basically been content with being an onlooker and occasionally cheering for someone." And with that insight, she decided to make some changes.

LOVE AND LOGIC
CHILDHOOD MATRIX

© Foster & Hermie Cline

MOTHER

FATHER

Name: _____

Name: _____

Age at your birth: ____

Age at your birth: ____

CHILDHOOD MATRIX

Adjectives:

Adjectives:

_____

_____

_____

_____

_____

_____

Most admired character
(real or fictional):

YOU
Your name and
nickname at age 11:

EPITAPHS

Mother: _____

_____

_____

_____

Father: _____

Favorite childhood
story, movie, TV
program:

_____

_____

Siblings, names and ages
when you were age 11:

Father: _____

_____

_____

Self: _____

_____

_____

Major messages between
you and your siblings:

R.I.P.

_____

_____

Instructions for Filling Out the Matrix Diagram

In the upper left corner, fill in your mother's name and the adjectives that described her in your childhood. In the upper right corner fill in your father's name and the adjectives that best described him. Because the matrix involves issues that are close to us, it may be difficult to think of adjectives. There may be a little unconscious blocking. Let's explore this a bit. Certainly, if asked to give adjectives that best describe a neighbor or acquaintance, most of you would have no trouble. But parents? Hum!? That can be a horse of a different color. But when describing a parent, some individuals draw a complete blank. If that happens to you, stick with the program. Relax. Maybe there is something there that is difficult to look at. Well, join the human race!

Many of you have had more than one mother or father figure. If that is the case, pick the one you feel was most influential in your childhood. Or if, for instance, your mother had a series of boyfriends and settled down with one, you may want to pick a "composite man" as the father figure. If you had no mother or father figure at all, just write the word "empty" to clarify that situation.

At the bottom of the triangle, write the name you were called as a child. If you had siblings who played an important part in your life, write their names under yours.

Note the lines that denote major statements going back and forth between your mother and father, and between you and your parents. These major statements are often unspoken messages that were "in the air" a great deal of the time. Here are some sample major messages that many individuals have noted were passed back and forth between their parents:

I love you. <—> I love you.

I love you. <—> Well, you don't show it!

You never pay attention to me. <—> That's not true.

You're always drunk. <—> Don't start that on me.

You don't care what I think. <—> I've had a hard day.

Notice also there are lines between each parent and the child. Write along those lines the messages that passed back and forth between you and your parents. Again, these messages may have been "in the air" and not necessarily said verbally. For instance, one of my dad's favorite messages was, "Hit 'em hard and don't bounce back." Another one was, "It's better to be a large fish in a small pond than a small fish in a large pond."

Likewise, write the major messages between you and the siblings who were important in your life.

At the bottom right of the diagram, above the tombstone, fill in the epitaphs that would sum up your mother's, your father's and your own life. At the bottom left, fill in the name of your hero. That is, anyone in *fiction or history* whose life you would like to have lived. Such a real or fictional person really tells something about your goals and desires.

Note that you are to fill in your "favorite" childhood story, movie or television program. Don't take a long time figuring out which was your favorite. *You will learn more if you take the first one that comes to mind!* This can also give you surprising clues about your life and unconscious self.

Discussing Your Matrix with Your Spouse

As we said, this experience can be a real eye-opener. So be gentle with each other and take it slow. Go over the messages and adjectives with care, taking turns. And no judgmental statements like, "Gees, no wonder you are always late." When partners in the relationship do this thoughtfully, without rushing through it, exploring what it means for their relationship, the matrix can be most enlightening.

View the video "Exploring Your Childhood Matrix." Amy and Rob do a good job of showing how to profit or not profit from this exercise.

COUPLE MESSAGES

Now that you've completed the *Childhood Matrix*, spend a little more time with each other and discuss the messages that go back and forth between the two of you. On the next page, fill in the form *Our Three Major Messages*. Add the adjectives that best describe each of you now and the major messages that you pass back and forth, often unspoken of course. You may find some interesting parallels with the things you discovered in the *Childhood Matrix*. A fun variation is to fill it out as you feel your spouse would fill it out.

If you have grown children or teens, you should find it enlightening to write the messages you feel are being sent back and forth between all family members. If your children are grown, you may want to include them or share the *Childhood Matrix* with them. Grown children, by the way, almost inevitably find the experience enlightening. And just imagine what you might learn when your grown or older children fill it out and share it with you!

Younger teens may generally be a little more reluctant to fill out the matrix. Maybe it's just too close to home and they don't have the perspective. It depends on your teens and their maturity level and their relationship with you.

If more than two of you participate in this exercise, make extra copies of the form.

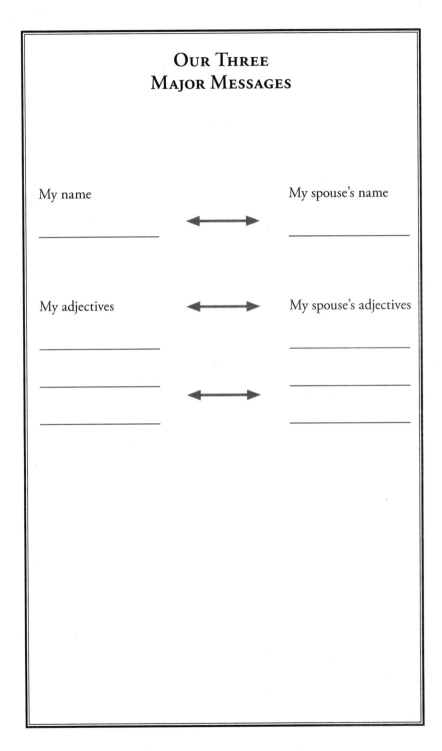

OUR THREE
MAJOR MESSAGES

My name

My spouse's name

_____

_____

My adjectives

My spouse's adjectives

_____

_____

_____

_____

Keeping
Romance Alive

When You Get Down to It, What Is Romance?

SOME HAPPY and perhaps fairly rare marriages manage to keep the romance alive. *Romance*—an easy term, but what does it really mean? What is the definition of romance? Is it sex, fascination, infatuation, communication, love, genuine interest or some kind of combination?

Certainly most everyone agrees that *romance is a special quality that keeps the relationship constantly renewed, energized and strengthened.* It ensures that the relationship does not become boring, stale and predictable. Romance has little to do with sexuality per se, but a lot to do with love and caring. *Romance is love with spice. Romance adds flavor to a relationship.*

Romance is renewing because of its special components. It is essential to define these components. If you don't first define something, you can't strive for it.

The Ingredients of Romance

Love is an essential element of romance. But that in itself is hard to define. Love can grow out of the ashes of disappointment or the fire of a sexual experience. Probably it is best to stick with the 1 Corinthians definition given earlier. Part of romance is giving, but material gifts offered without the essence of love are simply received as manipulative or meaningless.

Creativity is a sign that thought has been given to the romantic gift. (And creativity, incidentally, is a sign of intelligence.) When we are romanced with creativity, it is a doubly good indication. We have both a caring and an imaginative partner!

Surprise is a very important aspect of the romantic moment—it's stimulating, and keeps the neurons alive! Many romantic moments have an element of surprise. There are, of course, many different types of surprises. A loveless surprise is not romantic. Surprise demands *initiative!* Thus, a young wife talked to us about her husband romancing her: "It's so romantic when he actually dreams up an event and springs it on me! There is something about his doing it all by himself that is so appealing and exciting!"

Giving of self is an element of romance. The giving of self does not have to be extensive or expensive. It may be a material gift, or more important, a gift of time, attention or energy. Many couple relationships flounder simply because the gift of time is not given.

It is surprising that romance can often be ruined by sex. Sex that is demanding or sex that does not take the loved one's desires into account is actually the opposite of romance! People may want sex at different times. In some marriages, when she wants it, he doesn't; when he wants it, she doesn't; and occasionally, but not too often, they both want it at the same time. A common problem in such relationships, especially if one wants sex more than the other, is that a lack of touch and affection can develop. The one that doesn't want sex is afraid to be responsive to touch and affection for fear that it will simply be read as a covert agreement to sex. Or that it will be perceived as a preamble that leads to a more extensive experience. And such assumptions may or may not be true. In fact, couples can often agree to simply enjoy cuddling together with a mutual understanding that such receptiveness to touch and affection isn't a covert contract for sex; paradoxically, or perhaps not, when couples adhere to such an agreement, they often experience a closer relationship, which might lead to more *mutually encouraged* sex!

Many of our couples have found romance in the ideas below:

Giving

Flowers

Notes around the house, and in unexpected places

An unexpected evening out

An unexpected gift of time for one's partner

A bubble bath and massage

A house cleaning

An evening roasting marshmallows at a fire

Coupons or certificates to be "cashed in"

Bringing coffee or breakfast in bed

Unexpected baby-sitting for the children

Spreading a blanket in the park under a tree

Offering an unexpected glass of wine in the evening

Reading to each other

Creativity

Body painting

Unexpected trips and activities

Unexpected poems and prose

An unexpected sketch or drawing

Showing Romantic Creativity in Two Ways

There are two basic ways to show romantic creativity:

1. Meeting the *other's* needs: "I know you like eggplant."
   What would my partner really want and be shocked or surprised
      to receive?
   Requires giving on the part of the person presenting the
      romantic event.
2. Sharing of *ourselves*: "I wanted to show you my favorite fishing hole."
   Find something that excites you and share that excitement with
      your partner.
   Requires acceptance by the person receiving the romantic event.

Giving What Excites the Other

The year before Hermie's fiftieth birthday, I talked to a travel agent in order to find the perfect resort in Mexico: a place on the beach that friends could afford for a week. Finally, a Cozumel resort was chosen. I set up a special and secret bank account because Hermie takes care of the books. And money for this trip flowed into and out of that account. Friends and family were notified of the time and given group rates. A travel agent did all the coordinating. I told her that we were going "someplace" for her birthday. When asked what kind of clothes she should pack, I replied that she should pack for a cold mountain climate, but that wherever she went she would be near a great indoor pool, so she should pack a swimming suit as well. I didn't tell her when we would be leaving. And I left an Alaskan highway atlas out of sight, but where I knew she'd find it. Thus the anticipation built.

On the day that we left, I asked her if she'd mind helping me at the office for a while. On a prearranged signal all the employees present rose at once and shouted, "Goodbye, have a nice trip!" and I took her out to the parking lot, telling her that we were on our way to the *bus depot!*

"Where are we going to go on a *bus?*" she asked in dismay. "What about clothes? I can't go anywhere looking like *this!*"

Then to her surprise, I drove right by the bus depot and went on to the *train station. But I passed that too and ended up at the airport!*

We were met there by our grown children, one of whom had retrieved (by prearrangement) the suitcases that had been packed with the idea of going somewhere, sometime. Our kids walked us to the gate to see us off.

The next shock occurred when our grown children and their spouses, rather than just coming to bid goodbye at the gate, actually got on the plane! Then Hermie found that more of our friends had booked the same flight.

A final surprise occurred when more old friends and relatives met us at the resort. There, one of them waited on our table on the first night, unrecognized because he wore a huge sombrero and false mustache. Nothing Hermie ordered was available: "I'm so sorry, Señora, we just do not have that in."

Finally, everyone could not contain their laughter and she recognized my brother. The kind of high I received from that little romantic caper has been worth years of memories.

Giving What Excites Me

Hermie and I discussed buying a hot tub. She *really* wanted one, but I thought it could just end up being a waste of electric energy. When I returned home from a winter meeting late one night she was gone. But she'd left a note.

"Not home right now, Dear. But welcome home anyway! There's a package for you under the message on your desk." Walking to my desk, I found a huge white box containing a robe beneath another note. The new message read, "Please put on this robe and look in the pocket." I stripped down and put on the robe as directed. In the pocket, I found another note, which read, "Go look in the bathroom shower." In the shower I found a folded towel and another note: "Take the towel and go out on the deck and look around." I did, and there she was, waiting in the new hot tub with two glasses of wine and a smile.

Over the remainder of the evening I came to the conclusion that having a hot tub was really a pretty good idea and I have continued to appreciate something I would never have chosen for us or myself in the first place. "Oh wise wife, you were right again!"

However, a romantic moment need not be a production. A man in one of our groups told the following story: "I was on the Wave Runner, and turned too sharply and fell into the lake. Mary came up in her Wave Runner, dived in and swam over just to give me a kiss! Now I call that romantic!"

Romance may be just showing attention with prolonged eye contact and touching. Maggie summed it up: "When he starts whispering, I start listening!"

Exploring Romance Communication

You will need a couple of copies of the following questionnaire, one for each of you.

1. What is the most romantic experience you have initiated in the relationship?

_____

_____

2. What is the most romantic experience initiated by your partner in your relationship?

_____

_____

3. Guess the answers your partner would give to questions 1 and 2 above.

_____

_____

4. What are your partner's favorite activities?

_____

_____

5. What can you do to surprise and facilitate an experience around that activity?

_____

_____

6. What are the aspects you would most cherish in a romantic experience?

_____

_____

7. What are the activities that *your partner* would most cherish in a romantic experience?

_____

_____

ROMANCE IN OUR RELATIONSHIP

You will need a couple of copies of the following questionnaire, one for each of you.

1. Rate the amount of romance in your relationship from 0% to 100%.

   (0% = "There is not one iota of romance in our relationship.")
   (100% = "We are romantic with each other just the right amount.")

   Romance percentage: _____

2. The amount of romance in the relationship, however much or little, is still 100% of the romance shown. What percentage of the romance shown is initiated by:

   You: _____
   Your partner: _____

3. If the romance in our relationship were to improve, it would most likely be because ... (use only one sentence)

   _____

   _____

   _____

   _____

   _____

4. I feel _____ % happy, overall, with our romance.

5. The thing I like best about our relationship is ... (only one sentence)

   _____

   _____

   _____

   _____

6. Very likely, you would want to change at least one to three things in your relationship to make it better. List these individually, in order of preference. Be specific! For instance, it won't help to say, "We need to communicate better." It's more specific to write something like, "I would like us to spend one hour twice a week talking together" or "I wish I were not so defensive when my partner is critical."

(a) _____

(b) _____

(c) _____

7. Mark each of the answers above with an *S* for "self" and an *O* for "other" on the changes you or your partner must make to take primary responsibility.

8. From 0% to 100%, mark after each answer in question 6 what you think are the *actual chances* of the above changes occurring within three months, provided an honest effort is made by whoever needs to make it. If you feel it's not possible to make an honest effort, you must write *0%*.

9. At this point, would you like to reconsider the percentages you wrote down in question 2?

10. What three qualities do you most appreciate in your partner? (one-word descriptives)

(a) _____

(b) _____

(c) _____

If you'd like to see how well you communicate and how well you know each other, answer all of these questions again as you feel they would be answered by your spouse.

11

The Marriage Magic Will Continue ...

Summing Up

We named this chapter "The Marriage Magic Will Continue ..." because it's the end of the book, but not the end of the magic you will continue to share with each other.

By now it is obvious that good relationships don't "just happen." A relationship is a living thing, and nothing alive "just happens." Life means constant change and needs ongoing nutrition to be sustained or promote growth.

Your relationship is like a garden. Gardens don't just happen. And the results of tilling and planting are never immediate. The garden only becomes awesome with the passing of seasons. You must wait and be patient. Although it is almost always eventually productive and beautiful, the seasons always have their surprising way of bringing the unexpected. Just as Hermie and I have, you will be likely to experience the frost of unanticipated deaths in the family, the heartbreak when your garden is trampled by some unexpected mammal that wanders though your couple relationship, and there will probably be times of drought when finances are really tight.

You know how it is with that old garden. You scurry about the house with your mind caught up in all the day-to-day things that you do, but that one thoughtful, squinty eye is always sort of cocked toward the window, watching the weather, casting about, checking what's growing. When you look at the fruit of your garden, you will wonder at times if those kids are apples or onions. But of all the things we can do in life, little is as fulfilling as tending a garden.

In the garden of your relationship, you have used the concepts and exercises in this book to till the soil and provide the bedding for future growth. The nutrition of Love and Logic tools and techniques has been spread and hopefully many seeds of growth have been planted. But don't kid yourself. Just because you've finished this book, it's not over. It's not over even when one of you dies and the memories of your times together stream across that old pillow at night and curl through the room of the one who remains. You'll probably be working on the relationship and what it *really* meant, in one way or another, until the last of you takes your last breath.

What a privilege it has been to be with you for part of your planting. Now that you have completed this book, you know that nothing can take the place of *focused* interaction, with the *intent* of exploring, learning and growing in your relationship. As a living thing, your marriage is an *evolving* garden of flowering emotions, the scent of which fills your psychic life. Continued happiness will be likely with your *awareness and willingness to use the tools and techniques you have learned to discuss and explore the new situations* that will surely arise. Sure, there will be both rain and sun in your futures, but rather than wander about getting soaked or burnt, you know how to respond with communication tools and problem solving. The rejoicing you do in the good times, when the sun comes out after the squall, will be enhanced by your recognition of your helpmate and soulmate relationships.

A Prescription for Your Future

Might I go back to my medical roots and leave you with a prescription? As an old doc, I know that compliance is a problem. Only a third of all prescriptions are taken as directed. I bet you can do better than that.

Every Day

- When you need to get yourself a salad fork or spoon because the table wasn't set with it, be sure to bring another for your spouse.
- When you pass your spouse, touch him or her.
- Husbands, always put down the toilet seat.
- Use "Please," "Thank you" and "I'm sorry" with utter abandon.

Every Week

Just the two of you should set aside a time to review:

- What was the most enjoyable experience this week?
- What was the most memorable experience this week?
- What do you most hope will happen in the following week?
- What do you appreciate about your partner?
- What dreams or hopes can be shared?
- Catch up on the day-to-day happenings that have not been shared.

Once a Year

At least once a year, spend at least three days together on a vacation *free of the kids*. Sometime during your time alone, revisit a mutually agreeable *Love and Logic Experience*. You will be amazed at how some of your responses and ideas mature and change with time.

Every Five Years

Take a weekend just to focus on your relationship. This is not simply a vacation, where you both enjoy each other having fun. We are talking about a retreat that focuses specifically on your mutual goals, your mutual growth and your plans for the future. We are talking about a marriage retreat. Change facilitators, meet new people, enjoy new places.

Hermie and I encourage you to keep this book and the *Love and Logic Experiences* alive as a reference tool. We ask you to review it and come back to it on occasion. If you do that, you will find that those once-entrenched negative habits will melt away to be replaced by beauty and love expressed in ways you probably never thought possible.

As you revisit these exercises over time, you will see the great wisdom buried in these pages. You will see it in the quiet, loving smile on your spouse's face. You will find it in the little things you do for each other, creative things that make being together fun. You will find trust and depth where once the soil may have been shallow and uncertain.

Always remember that for healthy people, life is a win/win situation. And assuming you have a healthy partner, when your loved-one wins, you win. And your relationship wins. So focus on keeping that other person happy.

So don't put this book away. Choose instead to keep it around until others begin to see that something powerful has happened in your relationship. You will know you've succeeded when other people begin to comment on what you have. They will see the manifestations of fruit. When others see the beauty in your special garden, the garden of relationship that each of you has tended, they will comment on it because they'll wish your success for everyone.

Love and Logic Experiences

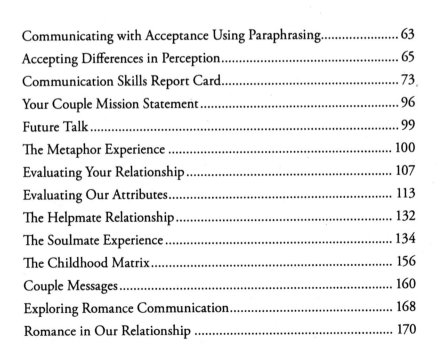

Contents of DVD

1   Introduction

2   Poor Communication

3   Correct Communication

4   The Need For Listening

5   The Importance of Listening

6   A Love & Logic Experience

7   Discuss Paraphrasing

8   Paraphrasing Correctly

9   Rules For Communication

10   Discussing the Rules of Communication Correctly

11   Your Mission Statement

12   Future Talk

13   Evaluating Your Relationship

14   Your Help Mate Relationship

15   Exploring Your Childhood Matrix

16   Bloopers

17   Link to Love and Logic Couples Evaluation

About the Authors

FOSTER AND HERMIE CLINE married in 1960 after meeting as freshmen while attending the University of Colorado in Boulder. During their marriage and parenting years they have raised three birth children and a child adopted at age eight. During those years they also parented three foster children for a time. Hermie also stayed busy with the CU wives group, both in Boulder and in Denver, worked in a doctor's office in Washington, worked with the Boy Scouts and the Evergreen Chorale, and did bookkeeping for the family business, volunteer work and quilting. All the while, she assisted Foster in their work with couples.

Foster graduated from the University of Colorado in 1962 and the family moved to Denver, where he attended the University of Colorado Medical School, graduating in 1966. After a medical internship at the federal hospital in the Panama Canal Zone, the family moved to Mercer Island, Washington, where they lived during Foster's adult and child psychiatric residency at the University of Washington in Seattle. Following that, the Clines returned to Colorado. They lived in Evergreen, where Foster had an extensive private practice in adult and child psychiatry. Foster now travels extensively, lecturing to groups across the country.

During that time Foster and his longtime friend, Jim Fay, founded the Cline/Fay Institute, which now operates as the Love and Logic Institute. The two of them have authored a number of outstanding books together, including *Parenting with Love and Logic, Parenting Teens with Love and Logic* and *Grandparenting with Love and Logic*. Additionally, Foster has written a number of other books, many for therapists and educators.

Foster and Hermie have facilitated couple groups and couple retreats since the early 1970s for numerous organizations throughout the United States and in many foreign countries. For years, they facilitated a weekly couples group and monthly weekend retreats in the mountains of Colorado.

Index